Emma

Howard Zinn

Emma

A Play in Two Acts
About Emma Goldman,
American Anarchist

Haymarket Books
Chicago, IL

© 1986 and 2002 by Howard Zinn

First published in 2002 by South End Press.
This edition published in 2013 by Haymarket Books.
P.O. Box 180165
Chicago, IL 60618
773-583-7884
info@haymarketbooks.org
www.haymarketbooks.org

ISBN: 978-1-60846-307-7

Trade distribution:
In the U.S. through Consortium Book Sales and Distribution, www.cbsd.com
In the UK, Turnaround Publisher Services, www.turnaround-uk.com
In Canada, Publishers Group Canada, www.pgcbooks.ca
In Australia, Palgrave Macmillan, www.palgravemacmillan.com.au
All other countries, Ingram Publisher Services International, ips_intlsales@
ingramcontent.com

Special discounts are available for bulk purchases by organizations
and institutions. Please contact Haymarket Books for more information
at 773-583-7884 or info@haymarketbooks.org.

This book was published with the generous support of
the Wallace Global Fund and Lannan Foundation.

Entered into digital printing February 2018.

Library of Congress CIP Data is available.

TABLE OF CONTENTS

INTRODUCTION

I was introduced to Emma Goldman (though not personally) by a fellow historian, Richard Drinnon, whom I met at a conference in Pennsylvania in the early 1960s. He told me he had written a biography of her called *Rebel in Paradise*.[1] When I returned home, I found the book and read it, more and more fascinated by this astonishing figure in American history. It struck me that in all of my work in American history, whether in undergraduate or graduate school, her name had never come up.

This was an experience I was to have many times after I left school and began to read about people and events that somehow never fit into the traditional history curriculum: Mother Jones, Big Bill Haywood, John Reed, the Ludlow Massacre, the Lawrence Textile Strike, the Haymarket Affair, and much more. The people it was considered important to study were presidents, industrialists, military heroes—not labor leaders, radicals, socialists, anarchists. Emma Goldman did not fit.

I was led to read Emma's autobiography, *Living My Life*.[2] Then I turned to the works of the Russian anarchists Peter Kropotkin and Mikhail Bakunin.[3] I became interested in anarchism as a political philosophy, and discovered that it was outside the pale of orthodox political theory as taught in the academic world. Coming to the faculty of Boston University in the fall of 1964, I was introduced to another new faculty member whose field was philosophy. Learning that I was joining the political science department, he asked: "And what is your political philosophy?" I replied, half-seriously, "Anarchism." He looked at me sharply and said: "Impossible!"

In 1974, while I was teaching in Paris, I made a trip to Amsterdam, and visited the International Institute of Social History. There I found a treasure trove of letters between Emma Goldman and Alexander Berkman, written in Europe after they were deported from the United States at the close of the first World War. I copied as much as I could on rough pieces of note paper, but when I returned home I found that Richard and Anna Maria Drinnon had gone through the same material and had just published a selection of the Goldman–Berkman correspondence, by the title *Nowhere at Home*.[4]

Through the 1960s and early 1970s, much of my life had been taken up with the movement against the war in Vietnam—speaking, participating in demonstrations, traveling to Japan and to Vietnam, writing about the

American invasion of Southeast Asia. When the war ended in 1975, I finally found time to do what I had been wanting to do for a long time, to write a play about the magnificent Emma Goldman. My son, Jeff, an actor given his first directing assignment by the Theater for the New City in Manhattan, offered to direct the first production of the play in 1976.

The following year, rewritten (as it has been after every production), it played in Boston, directed by Maxine Klein, with the ensemble group "The Next Move" forming the cast. It received glowing reviews, played for eight months, and was seen by about 20,000 people. In the years that followed, it played again in New York, then in London and in Tokyo. One version of it was published by the South End Press as part of a collection of feminist plays called *Playbook*.[5] The play, of necessity, can only cover a part of Emma Goldman's remarkable life story. She was born in Kovno, Lithuania, which was then part of Russia, in 1869, and in her memoir recalls both the miseries of life in a poor Jewish family and the rare moments of excitement that punctuated that life. Always open to passionate encounters, she tells of her first erotic experience, as a little girl being thrown into the air and caught again and again by a young man of the village. She tells also of being taken to the opera while visiting a prosperous aunt in Konigsberg, and weeping as one of Verdi's beautiful arias filled the concert hall.

Her family emigrated to the United States, and lived in Rochester, New York, amidst the Jewish immigrant culture. At sixteen, Emma was working in a factory. She was abruptly married off to a young man she did not love and who was unable to consummate the marriage. Her father was a tyrant. So she learned early of the subordination of women, to husbands, to fathers. But she was a reader, and a dreamer. At seventeen, she became aware of the labor struggles in Chicago for an eight-hour day. In these struggles, the Haymarket Affair of 1886 played a central role.

Its origin was in a strike against the International Harvester Company, during which police killed several strikers. The anarchist movement in Chicago, which was formidable, called for a protest meeting in Haymarket Square. The meeting was peaceful, but when a small army of police decided to break it up, a bomb exploded in the police ranks, wounding sixty-six policemen, of whom seven later died. The police then fired into the crowd, killing several people, and wounding two hundred.

There was no evidence on who threw the bomb (and to this day it remains a mystery), but the police arrested eight anarchist leaders in Chicago. A jury found them guilty, on the supposition that whoever threw the bomb must have been influenced by the incendiary statements of the anarchists, whose circulars, after the International

Harvester shootings, called for "Revenge!" The eight were sentenced to death by hanging.

This became an event of international excitement. Meetings took place all over Europe in defense of the condemned men. When their appeal was turned down by the Illinois Supreme Court, George Bernard Shaw responded: "If the world must lose eight of its people, it can better afford to lose the eight members of the Illinois Supreme Court." One of the men blew himself up in his cell. Three were later pardoned by Governor John Peter Altgeld of Illinois (who later became the subject of a historical novel by Howard Fast called *The American*).[6] Four were hanged.

These events had a tumultuous emotional effect on the young Emma. She decided to leave her family in Rochester, leave her job and her husband behind, and go to New York, where she could find the freedom to live her own life. There she met a group of young anarchists, among them Alexander Berkman, also an immigrant from Russia, and ferociously devoted to the cause of creating a new society. Emma and Sasha (as Berkman was known to his friends) became lovers.

A powerful influence on both Emma and Sasha was the famous German revolutionary, Johann Most, who had been in the Reichstag, had spent time in prison, and now used his eloquence on the public platform to advance the cause of anarchism. Most was taken with the young, passionate comrade, and this led to some tension between Emma and Sasha.

Emma found work in a factory and began organizing the immigrant workers (most of them women) in Manhattan. In 1892, workers in Homestead, Pennsylvania, initiated a strike against one of Andrew Carnegie's steel mills, managed by the ruthless Henry Clay Frick (later to become, like Carnegie, a philanthropist). Frick hired the Pinkerton Detective Agency, the largest strikebreaking agency in the nation, and at one point its operatives opened fire with rifles and machine guns, killing seven strikers.

Aroused by this, Emma and Sasha and several of their comrades decided on a bold act of vengeance, to show the world that the titans of industry were not invulnerable. They would assassinate Henry Clay Frick.

Sasha, willing to sacrifice himself for the good of the cause, insisted on carrying out the act alone. He traveled to Pittsburgh, burst into Frick's office, and fired away. Sasha was hardly an experienced assassin. His shots only managed to wound Frick, and he was overpowered. The trial was quick, and he was sentenced to twenty-two years in the Pennsylvania State Penitentiary. His account of that experience, *Prison Memoirs of an Anarchist*, is a classic of prison writing.[7]

Life in prison was an endless torment, especially since Sasha continued to defy the authorities in many ways and was repeatedly punished. Other prisoners had committed suicide rather than endure the cruelties of imprisonment, and Sasha was not sure he would last out his time. His desperation was conveyed to Emma and his friends, and they concocted a bizarre plan for his escape. They rented a house not far from the prison walls and began to dig a tunnel that would come up in the prison yard, with a comrade playing a piano to drown out the sounds of digging.

But just at the time they finished their work, the tunnel was discovered and Sasha was severely punished. While Berkman was in prison, Emma continued to organize and agitate. In 1893, a terrible year of economic crisis, when children in the cities were dying of hunger and sickness, she addressed a huge demonstration in Union Square and urged her listeners to invade the food stores and take what they needed to feed their families—rather than waiting for legislation or petitioning the authorities. This was a vivid illustration of the anarchist principle of "direct action." Emma was dragged off the speakers' platform by the police and was sentenced to two years on Blackwell's Island.

In prison, Emma learned nursing and midwifery. This training was to be useful for the rest of her life. (In E.L. Doctorow's novel *Ragtime*, there is a brilliantly written scene of Emma giving a massage to a showgirl of that era.)[8]

While Sasha was enduring prison, Emma was rapidly becoming known as a leading orator and organizer in the labor and anarchist movements.

When President William McKinley was shot and killed in 1901 by a man named Leon Czolgosz, Emma had to hide out because the police immediately, and mistakenly, assumed she was involved in the assassination.

In fact, Emma Goldman no longer believed, as she did at the time of the Frick event, that assassination was justified in the cause of anarchism, but she refused to heap abuse on Czolgosz, as some of her radical friends did, arguing that, however irrational his act, people had to understand that there were legitimate reasons for his anger.

Through all this time, in keeping with her philosophy of freedom in love, Emma had various lovers, even while she retained enormous affection and admiration for Alexander Berkman. When he finally came out of prison in 1906, their friendship was renewed, but they were no longer sexually intimate. They remained comrades in the cause of anarchism and together founded the journal *Mother Earth*.[9]

In 1908, while lecturing in Chicago, Emma encountered for the first time the amazing Ben Reitman, in what would become the most tumultuous emotional experience of her life. He was Dr. Ben Reitman, having made his way somehow through medical school, but he was as far from the traditional physician as one could imagine. He was dark-haired and handsome, a man who dressed flamboyantly and opened a storefront clinic in Chicago where hobos, prostitutes, and poor people in general could come for help. He performed abortions and otherwise flouted the rules of the profession and of society.

Reitman was a man of ferocious sexual appetites, and he and Emma fell passionately in love. Their correspondence, only discovered in recent years, is among the most torrid and explicit in the annals of letter-writing. She was 39 and he was 29, but the difference in age was clearly not important. In *Living My Life*, Emma describes meeting Reitman:

> He arrived in the afternoon, an exotic, picturesque figure with a large black cowboy hat, flowing silk tie, and huge cane.... His voice was deep, soft, and ingratiating.... [He was] a tall man with a finely shaped head, covered with a mass of curly black hair, which evidently had not been washed for some time. His eyes were brown, large, and dreamy. His lips, disclosing beautiful teeth when he smiled, were full and passionate. He looked a handsome brute.... I could not take my eyes off his hands.[10]

Shortly after meeting Reitman, Emma wrote to him: "You have opened up the prison gates of my womanhood.... [I]f I were asked to choose between a world of understanding and the spring that fills my body with fire, I should have to choose the spring."[11]

Emma was soon in thrall to her overwhelming physical need for Reitman. He was traveling with Emma, managing her lectures, but also ready for adventures with other women. Yet she could not break the tie. She wrote to him at one point:

> If ever our correspondence should be published, the world would stand aghast that I, Emma Goldman, the strong revolutionist, the daredevil, the one who has defied laws and convention, should have been as helpless as a shipwrecked crew on a foaming ocean.[12]

Yet Emma Goldman did not stop her endless speaking, agitating, organizing. She seemed to be tireless as she traveled the country, lecturing to large audiences everywhere, on birth control ("A woman should decide for herself"), on the problems of marriage as an institution ("Marriage has nothing to do with love"), on patriotism ("the last refuge of a scoundrel"), on free love ("What is love if not free?"), and also on the drama—Shaw, Ibsen, Strindberg.

She was arrested again and again, simply for speaking. In Chicago in 1908 police dragged her off the stage. A reporter for the Chicago *Daily Tribune* recorded this dialogue:

> "Thought you'd come here and make trouble, eh?"
> the Captain [said] …
> "Behave yourself," said Miss Goldman sharply. "Talk
> like a man, even if you are a policeman."[13]

In one month in 1909, police broke up eleven of her meetings. In San Francisco, she spoke to 5,000 people on patriotism, with the crowd blocking off the police until they retreated.[14] In San Diego, a mob kidnapped Ben Reitman, took him out of town, tarred and feathered him, and branded his buttocks with the initials "I.W.W." But (a tribute to his courage, as well as to hers) the two of them returned later to San Diego for Emma to give her talk.

Emma's sexual freedom may well have gone so far as to permit a brief erotic relationship with a woman in New Kensington, Pennsylvania. The woman was Almeda Sperry. Though she is not mentioned in Emma's autobiography, I came across a batch of letters from Almeda to Emma in the special collections of the Boston University Library.[15] Almeda was an extraordinary person, a working class woman who gave of her body to men when she needed money, who loved theater and opera, and who set up a socialist group in New Kensington.

Almeda Sperry's letters to Emma are remarkable for their passionate declarations of affections, their intense social consciousness, their insights into the life of a woman struggling to survive, and her exultant love for opera, theater, and literature. When I read them, I knew I must somehow recreate her presence in my play, even if only through one of her letters, as she describes an encounter with Ben Reitman. Here is a passage from another letter:

> I wonder if everyone is as dippy as I am about shows.... I almost committed suicide when Sara Bernhardt was to come here last and I was broke, but Fred gave me a dollar and I got a seat in goose heaven. What a voice Sara has—what a golden, liquid voice and what enunciation. I have practiced her rage in La Tosca in front of the looking glass.... Wouldn't it be grand, Emma, if the government would run the theatres and let the people in for nothing.... If I could go to a good show every night I'd work for just my grub and enuf clothes to hide my nakedness and I'd be kind to everybody.[16]

Reitman and Emma had ten tempestuous years together, during which Emma, despite her emotional turmoil, managed to maintain an extraordinary level of political activity, culminating in her opposition to American entrance into the war in 1917. That event also marked their breakup. Reitman, though he had shown personal courage in many ways, had no desire to risk his freedom by overt opposition to the war.

Emma and Alexander Berkman, comrades throughout it all, defied the law by denouncing conscription and the war, and were sentenced to prison in 1918. When the war was over, they were released, only to be deported, along with many other radicals, in the fierce repression that accompanied the war's end. At the start of his infamous career as a right-wing fanatic, J. Edgar Hoover himself supervised their deportation, on a boat bound for Russia, their birthplace.

It was no longer Tsarist Russia, however, but the new Soviet Union, in which Lenin had dissolved the Constituent Assembly, representing many political factions, and instituted the rule of the Bolsheviks. Emma and Sasha, meeting with Lenin and Trotsky, observing the jailing of dissidents, the breakup of demonstrations, and finally the bloody crushing of the sailors' revolt in Kronstadt, outside of Petrograd, could not bear the idea of remaining in the Soviet Union.

They spent their remaining years in various parts of Europe, especially on the Mediterranean coast of France, writing to one another endlessly (many of these letters are preserved in the collection by Richard and Anna Maria Drinnon), keeping in touch with events in Europe and the United States, lending their names and their support to whatever good causes moved them. Emma traveled to Spain during the civil war there and spoke in 1936 to enormous crowds in Barcelona, which was briefly an anarchist enclave (described vividly in George Orwell's *Homage to Catalonia*).[17]

Berkman, seriously ill and in pain, took his own life in 1936. Emma made a rare trip to the United States in 1940, through the offices of Frances Perkins, Roosevelt's progressive secretary of labor. The condition was that she only speak about the drama, and so she gave a series of lectures on Ibsen, Shaw, Strindberg, and Chekhov.[18] But, on a brief stop in Canada, she became ill and died. She was seventy-one.

The 1960s marked a revival of interest in anarchism. One reason was a fierce hostility to the American government. The federal government had collaborated for almost one hundred years in maintaining racial segregation in the South. That collaboration only came to an end (at least legally) when black people took to the streets in Georgia, Alabama, Mississippi, and the other Southern states, and embarrassed the nation before the entire world.

The same government was waging a brutal war in Southeast Asia, the longest war in the country's history. It only began to retreat from that in the face of fierce resistance in Vietnam and a huge national antiwar movement in the United States.

The radicals of the 1960s were not, like those of the 1930s, connected to the Communist movement or admirers of the Soviet Union. They called themselves "the New Left," and there was a strong ideological and emotional connection to anarchism, even though the term itself was not much used. The connection was not just a suspicion of all governments, but a belief in what the Students for a Democratic Society and others called "participatory democracy."

The movements of the 1960s seemed to embody the anarchist principle of decentralized organization, as opposed to the party discipline of the Old Left. The Student Nonviolent Coordinating Committee was made up of small groups, young and mostly black, working in the most dangerous parts of the deep South, embedding themselves in local communities, and maintaining only occasional contact with the national office in Atlanta.

The feminst movement of those years, also without talking about anarchism, acted on the anarchist principle of decentralized organization, working day by day in small women's groups throughout the country. From time to time, there would be parades and national demonstrations on behalf of sexual equality, but women were not bound to any one charismatic leader.

What also connected the movements of the 1960s to the historic philosophy of anarchism was the idea of direct action. This meant that social change would not be sought by political parties striving to take over government, but by citizens banding together and acting directly against the source of their oppression.

Historically, the labor movement, when it was not held back by conservative national leadership, had engaged in such action: strikes, directly against the employer, had won the eight-hour day. The government could not be counted on to do anything for working people. It was controlled by the rich and powerful, tied to corporate power. So workers had to do the job themselves.

The Southern civil rights movement used the slogan "nonviolent direct action" to describe its campaign of sit-ins and freedom rides. When antiwar activists blocked streets in Washington, D.C., surrounded the Pentagon, and broke into draft boards, they were engaging in direct action. The various acts of civil disobedience by dissidents, in challenging the law and the government, were consonant with anarchist philosophy, whether the participants knew this or not.

Anarchism as a philosophy, which had great influence in the late nineteenth and early twentieth centuries, in Europe and also in the United States, was overshadowed after 1917 by the Communist movement and its attachment to the Soviet Union. With the movements of the 1960s, this changed. The new antistate politics, as well as the culture of freedom, in music, in sex, in communal living, led to a revival of interest in anarchism.

Emma Goldman, after decades of obscurity, now became an admired figure, especially in the women's movement, but also in the other political and other movements of that time.

It was in the late 1960s that I began using anarchist writings in my course in political theory at Boston University. My students were reading Emma's autobiography, *Living My Life*, as well as a collection of her lectures, *Anarchsim and Other Essays*.[19] Sometimes I used a short book by Alexander Berkman, which was a concise and simple explanation of anarchist ideas, called *The ABC of Anarchism*.[20] I began teaching a seminar on "Marxism and Anarchism."

When the play *Emma* was first produced in New York and Boston, it covered the events of Emma Goldman's life up to the year 1906, when Alexander Berkman came out of prison. I knew about Emma's relationship with Ben Reitman, but when Candace Falk published her book *Love, Anarchy, and Emma Goldman*, reproducing the astonishing love letters between Emma and Ben, I felt I had to bring this swashbuckling character into my play.[21] And so, when the play was performed in London in 1987, Reitman became one of the characters, and the story was carried into the first World War.

For the English production, we changed the title of the play, because Jane Austen's novel *Emma* was so well known to English audiences. We now called the play *Rebel in Paradise*, with Richard Drinnon kindly consenting to our use of the title of his biography of Emma. When the play opened in Tokyo in 1990, we returned to the original title.

I have Anthony Arnove and South End Press to thank for publishing this edition of the play. Our hope is that this will make it more available to theater companies that might want to produce it.

1   Richard Drinnon, *Rebel in Paradise: A Biography of Emma Goldman* (Chicago: University of Chicago Press, 1961).

2   Emma Goldman, *Living My Life*, 2 vols. (New York: Dover Publications, 1970).

3   See Peter Kropotkin, *The Essential Kropotkin*, eds. Emile Capouya and Keitha Tompkins (New York: Liveright, 1975), and Mikhail Bakunin, *Mutual Aid: A Factor of Evolution*, ed. Paul Avrich (New York: New York University Press, 1972).

4   Emma Goldman and Alexander Berkman, *Nowhere at Home: Letters from Exile of Emma Goldman and Alexander Berkman*, eds. Richard and Anna Maria Drinnon (New York: Schocken Books, 1975).

5   Maxine Klein, Lydia Sargent, and Howard Zinn, *Playbook* (Boston: South End Press, 1986).

6   Howard Fast, *The American: A Middle Western Legend* (New York: Duell, Sloan, and Pearce, 1946).

7   Alexander Berkman, *Prison Memoirs of an Anarchist* (New York: New York Review of Books, 1999).

8   E.L. Doctorow, *Ragtime* (New York: Plume, 1996).

9   See Peter Glassgold, ed., *Anarchy! An Anthology of Emma Goldman's Mother Earth* (Washington, D.C.: Counterpoint, 2001).

10   Emma, *Living My Life*, vol. 1, pp. 415–416.

11   Candace Falk, *Love, Anarchy, and Emma Goldman* (New York: Holt, Rinehart, and Winston, 1984), p. 4.

12   Falk, *Love, Anarchy, and Emma Goldman*.

13   Falk, *Love, Anarchy, and Emma Goldman*, p. 65.

14   Goldman, *Living My Life*, vol. 1, 427–428. The talk, "Patriotism: A Menace to Liberty," appears in Goldman, *Anarchism and Other Essays*, pp. 127–144.

15   Boston University Library Special Collections, *Emma Goldman Papers*, Collection #243, Boxes 1, 2, 3. See also *The Emma Goldman Papers: A Microfilm Edition*, 69 reels (Ann Arbor, Michigan: Chadwyck-Healey, 1991), Reels, 6, 7, and 68; *Emma Goldman: A Guide to Her Life and Documentary Sources* (Ann Arbor, Michigan: Chadwyck-Healey, 1995); the forthcoming *Emma Goldman: A Documentary History of the American Years (1890–1919)—A Four-Volume Documentary Edition* (Berkeley: University of California Press, 2003); and the documents available at the Emma Goldman Papers Project, University of California, 2372 Ellsworth Street, Berkeley, CA 94720. Their web site is

http://sunsite.berkeley.edu/Goldman/ or e-mail emma@uclink.berkeley.edu.

16 See note 15 above.

17 George Orwell, *Homage to Catalonia* (New York: Harvest Books, 1987).

18 See Emma Goldman, *The Social Significance of the Modern Drama* (New York: Applause Theatre Book Publishers, 1987).

19 Goldman, *Anarchism and Other Essays*. See note 14 above.

20 Alexander Berkman, *The ABC of Anarchism* (London: Freedom Press, 1995).

21 Falk, *Love, Anarchy, and Emma Goldman*. See note 12 above.

SEQUENCE OF SCENES

Act One

1. The Factory
2. The Family
3. Sachs' Cafe
4. Johann Most Speaks
5. Anna's Apartment
6. Forming the Commune
7. Fedya and Emma
8. Strike at Kargman's
9. The Decision to Kill Frick
10. The Attempt

Act Two

Prologue: The Sentencing
1. Johann Most Speaks
2. Emma Meets Ben Reitman
3. Plan for Escape
4. Lecture Tour: Emma and Ben, Emma and Almeda
5. Union Square
6. J. Edgar Hoover
7. Emma in Prison: Letters
8. Speech at Thalia Theater
9. Birth: Emma and Helena
10. President McKinley: Reporters and Emma
11. Sasha Returns: Sachs' Cafe
12. Emma and Ben Part
13. The Harlem River Casino

CAST LIST

Emma Goldman: She is eighteen to twenty-two in Act One, twenty-two to thirty-seven in most of Act Two, forty-eight at end. Blue eyes, blonde or chestnut hair. Strong, pleasant features, voluptuous figure. Her temperament by turns fiery and gentle.

Alexander Berkman: Same age as Emma. Strongly built, bespectacled, scholarly face, serious demeanor.

Johann Most: In his forties, short black beard, short hair, face disfigured around his jaw, a powerful orator, capable of rousing a crowd, also biting in his wit.

Emma's Father, Act One, big, overbearing.

Frick (in shadows), Act One.

Ben Reitman: Act Two, in late twenties but looks older, a doctor in the Chicago slums, taking care of hobos, beggars, and prostitutes, a flamboyant character who wears flowing silk ties, a cowboy hat, and carries a cane. Handsome, dark hair, mustache.

Anna Minkin: Mostly in Act One, when she is in her twenties. Short, thin, a comic disposition, good singing voice.

Factory worker, Dora, Act One.

Emma's Mother, Taube Goldberg, Act One.

Factory worker, Jenny, Act One.

Prison nurse, Lizbeth, Act Two.

Almeda Sperry, Act Two.

Helena: Emma's sister, Act One and Act Two, a few years older than Emma.

Factory worker, Rose, Act One.

Fedya: Mostly in Act One, when he is in his twenties. Good looking, an artist, good singing voice, easygoing, gentle.

Vito: Mostly in Act One, in his twenties, a comedian of sorts, good singing voice.

Vogel, the Foreman, Act One.

Mr. Levine, Act One.

Mr. Sachs: Cafe owner, in his forties in Act One.

J. Edgar Hoover, Act Two. Young, stocky.

Thomas Gregory, Act Two.

Reporters, Act Two.

Voices, Act Two.

Pianist: There is music throughout; consult the score on tape for reference.

PRODUCTION HISTORY

New York, 1976, Theater for the New City, directed by Jeff Zinn.

Boston, 1977, The Next Move Theater, directed by Maxine Klein.

New York, 1986, Tomi Theater, directed by Maxine Klein.

London, 1987, Young Vic Theater, directed by Paulette Randall.

Edinburgh Festival, 1987, directed by Paulette Randall.

ACT ONE

SCENE 1: THE FACTORY

Overture: "Mein Ruhe Platz," on the piano, or, if taped, sung in chorus.

A factory whistle is heard in the dark. As the lights come up, four women, of various ages—Emma, Rose, Jenny, Dora—are sitting at the imaginary machines, going through the motions of sewing, their feet working the treadle, making a steady beat on the floor, their bodies going forward and back from the waist up, one hand working the material through, the other hand turning the wheel, and every few turns, without losing the rhythm, quickly wiping the sweat from their foreheads. They work silently, quickly, with excruciating regularity, and the only sound we hear is the rhythmic sound of feet on the floor, simulating the treadle. Then one of the women begins to sing "Mein Ruhe Platz." She sings two stanzas, and then the foreman, Vogel, appears—or his voice is heard offstage—an excitable man, not unkind but fearful and nervous about his responsibility.

VOGEL

How many times do I have to tell you? No singing on the job. Please! (The woman stops singing.) Who wants to sing, get a job with the opera! (He shakes his head, leaves. They continue working in silence. When they do speak, they do it without breaking the work rhythm.)

JENNY

You remember the fire at Kachinsky's shop last month?

DORA

Eighteen girls died. Some burned to death. Some jumped from windows. Who can forget such a thing?

JENNY

Well, it said in the paper this morning why those girls couldn't get down the back stairs.

DORA

So?

JENNY

The door was locked from the outside. Kachinsky locked it because a few girls were sneaking out on the roof for a little air.

DORA

The dirty bastard! And he calls himself a Jew.

ROSE

Is a Jewish boss any different?

DORA

A Jew is supposed to be different.

ROSE

They're all the same, believe me. I've worked for Jews, Gentiles—even Italians.

JENNY

I don't feel good working here on the eighth floor. There's too many fires these days. Did you read what the fire chief of New York said?

ROSE

Who reads all that foolishness?

JENNY

You better read. He says his ladders only reach up to the sixth floor. If you're on the seventh or eighth, like us, pray to God. (They all stop working the machines, there is no motion, no sound for a few seconds, then slowly they start up again.)

ROSE

You know the back door on this floor is locked from the outside, too—

JENNY

What are you saying?

ROSE

It's been that way ever since I've been working here.

DORA

That's not right.

ROSE

It's better not to think about it.

JENNY

Someone should tell Vogel to open the door.

DORA

You talk, you get in trouble. Who'll tell Vogel? Not me. (They keep working in silence.)

EMMA

(Loudly, startling the others) Mr. Vogel! Please! Go outside and open the back door. In case of a fire ...

VOGEL

(His voice offstage, a man who gets excited quickly) Mind your own business! You work on the corsets. It's Mr. Handlin's shop. I have nothing to do with doors. Emma, take my advice. You're the youngest girl here. Learn to mind your own business.

EMMA

(Getting up from the machine) I'm not working if the door is locked.

VOGEL

(Even more excited now) Good! Good! Leave! Go home right now. Who needs you? (He is a great gesticulator.) Dora, you stay a little later tonight and do Emma's work. You'll get paid extra. We have to finish this order tonight. Mr. Handlin is waiting for it.

DORA

(Softly) I can't stay later.

VOGEL

(Pointing) You, Jenny.

JENNY

I have to be home on time tonight.

VOGEL

(Desperately) Rose! (Rose shakes her head. Vogel is shouting now.) What's the matter with all of you?

ROSE

The door. You have to open the door.

VOGEL

I'm not supposed to. It's not my business. (Emma starts to leave.)

DORA

Emma, wait for me. (She gets up from the machine.) Mr. Vogel, I'm sorry, I'm scared of fires.

JENNY

Me, too. (She gets up.)

ROSE

Mr. Vogel, if there's a fire, you won't be able to get down the stairs either.

VOGEL

You're all *meshugah!* (They've all stopped working.) What are you doing to me? Please, girls. I've got a family to support. Please, back to the machines, the order has to get out tonight.

EMMA

Open the door!

ALL

Open the door!

VOGEL

(Shouting) All right! Enough! All right! (He goes off. We hear the sound of the latch opening and Vogel still shouting.) You're satisfied? I'll lose my job and then you'll be satisfied! All right, back to work! (They go back to the rhythm of the machines, working silently, only the sound of their shoes on the floor. Then, after the silence ...)

DORA

A friend of mine saw the fire at Kachinsky's shop ... (Everyone keeps working in silence.) The girls on the tenth floor came out on the window ledge, the flames all around them. They looked so small up there. And when their clothes began to burn, they jumped. Two of them, three of them, at a time—holding hands ... (Silence, as they work the machines. Then one of them starts humming "Mein Ruhe Platz" and the others join in, one by one, all humming and working the machines as the scene ends.)

SCENE 2: THE FAMILY

In the darkness, a happy Yiddish tune. Lights up on the Goldman kitchen. Emma and her sister, Helena, are dancing. Helena teaching Emma, both laughing. Mother preparing food. Father nodding his head to the music. Mr. Levine, a well-off distant relative in the dress business, enters.

FATHER

Hello, Mr. Levine! Emma … (She turns.) Stop dancing and say hello to Mr. Levine. Helena, you too! (Their faces show their distaste for Levine as they look at one another as if to say: "There he is again.")

LEVINE

(Embracing the girls, a little too tightly) Ah, your beautiful daughters! Hello, everybody.

FATHER

Sit down, sit down. Girls, go help your mother. (The girls go off to the side where their mother is, to help her, and to have fun, whispering "Mr. Levine is here!" Then pinching and fondling one another and laughing.) Taube! (Calling his wife) Taube, where's the soup? (Emma imitates him in whispers for Helena's benefit: "Taube, where's the soup?") What are you talking about there, you two? Come and sit down like people. (They bring the soup and sit at the far end of the table.)

LEVINE

Mrs. Goldman, how are you liking Rochester?

FATHER

(Answering for her) It's a thousand times better than New York.

EMMA

(Carrying on her own whispering conversation with Helena at the end of the table) Our mother cannot speak for herself!

HELENA

Father knows her mind best! (They've been through this before.)

FATHER

Here, in Rochester, you see a flower, a blade of grass …

EMMA

One flower, one blade of grass … (Helena giggles.)

FATHER

It's not so crowded here as in New York …

EMMA

Only seven in one room …

FATHER

(Sternly) No secrets there, girls! Be polite!

LEVINE

Was it hard finding work here?

FATHER

Oh, no, not hard at all. (The girls are making faces like: "No, not hard at all!" He turns to them, annoyed.) What are you two making those noises for? Don't you know how to sit at a table? (Then, to Levine) You know Jacob, Emma's husband. He has a good job. A big factory. They make beds.

EMMA

(Speaking up this time) Six dollars a week. Twelve hours a day. He isn't home yet.

FATHER

(Ignoring that) Emma has a job, too. In the garment district. Emma, tell Mr. Levine about your job.

EMMA

What's to tell? The place stinks. (Helena giggles.) Two dollars and fifty cents a week. We aren't allowed to sing. We aren't allowed to talk. The foreman tries to put his hands on the girls, so I have to give him a *zetz* in the face. (She demonstrates—Helena giggles.) Well (shrugging) I'm not allowed to *talk*.

FATHER

What a mouth on her! She goes to these meetings, and she listens to these socialists, communists, anarchists, who knows what they are? She doesn't realize what we all went through in the old country.

EMMA

I worked in a factory there, too, Papa. It's no different, except here you have to work faster.

FATHER

(Angrily) Here they don't kill Jews!

EMMA

They don't have to. The Jews kill themselves, on the machines.

FATHER

Here we have a place to live. Knock wood! (He raps on the table.)

EMMA

Yes, wood. It burns fast. Last week, down the street, a whole family burned to death. You think that happens to Rockefeller in his stone mansion?

LEVINE

At least we have firemen here. Who knew from firemen in the old country?

EMMA

That's America. Here are the most firemen, and the most fires.

FATHER

(Heatedly) We're lucky to be in Rochester. Where is it better, in New York? Packed into the tenements? The children dying of diphtheria, smallpox?

EMMA

At least, in New York, people are protesting ...

FATHER

All right! Go to New York, where all those *trumbenicks* are! Lazy slobs—they loaf around and then they scream, "America is no good." They don't appreciate this country. (He bangs the table. Everyone is silent.)

MOTHER

(Heading off an outburst) Emma, serve the soup. (Emma starts serving.)

LEVINE

(Trying to change the subject) I brought you the Yiddish newspaper.

FATHER

Thanks, thanks. So what's news?

LEVINE

You remember those fellows who threw the bomb in Chicago last year and killed all those policemen?

EMMA

(Loudly, firmly) No one ever found out who threw the bomb. So they arrested eight anarchist organizers: a printer, an upholsterer, a carpenter ...

FATHER

See—everything she knows. All right now, quiet while Mr. Levine is talking.

LEVINE

I'm just telling what's in the paper. Yesterday, they hanged four of them. (Emma sobs. Helena puts her arm around her.)

FATHER

What are you crying for?

LEVINE

They were anarchists. They had it coming to them.

EMMA

(Shouting) Shut up!

FATHER

(Standing, threatening) Respect!

LEVINE

(Not wanting to make trouble, but needing to say something, shrugs) What's to cry about? They were murderers.

EMMA

Shut your mouth! (She lifts a plate of soup and throws the soup into Mr. Levine's face. Father starts after her, pulling at his belt. Her mother gets between them.)

MOTHER

She's upset! She's upset!

EMMA

You touch me and you'll get it right back!

FATHER

(Enraged) What did you say?

EMMA

You heard me!

FATHER

(Lifting the strap) I'll teach her.

MOTHER

Helena, take her away before her father kills her. (Helena pulls Emma away. Mother hands Levine a towel to wipe his face.)

FATHER

That girl is crazy, out of her mind!

MOTHER

Shhh! Shhh! (Lights down on the kitchen, then up again on Emma and Helena sitting on a cot in the corner, a faint light, music "Mein Ruhe Platz," barely audible in the background.)

EMMA

Sleep with me, Helena.

HELENA

Isn't Jacob going to sleep with you?

EMMA

We don't sleep together. Not since the first night. I should never have married him.

> HELENA

Why did you?

> EMMA

I was lonely.

> HELENA

That's not a good reason.

> EMMA

And stupid.

> HELENA

That's a good reason.

> EMMA

But no more. I have to live my own life. I've made up my mind. I'm going to New York.

> HELENA

You're leaving Jacob, the family, your job?

> EMMA

Everything.

> HELENA

I wish I had your nerve.

> EMMA

You like your husband. Why should you leave?

HELENA

If I had more nerve, I wouldn't like him so much. (They both laugh, then are quiet, then Helena starts to laugh again.)

EMMA

What's so funny?

HELENA

The soup! Did you see Papa's face?

EMMA

Did you see Mr. Levine's face? (They both laugh. Then they are silent.) You know, Helena, I love you.

HELENA

(Holding back tears) You take care of yourself in New York. You heard what Papa said. That's where all the *trumbenicks* are! (They embrace, laughing, crying, as lights go down, music still faintly heard.)

SCENE 3: SACHS' CAFE

Lower Manhattan. A piano player. Mood of exuberance. Young people eating, drinking beer. Two tables. A hot August day. Mr. Sachs is playing the Italian game Morra with the pianist between numbers, throwing fingers in the air, calling out ...

SACHS

Quattro! Due! Otto! Uno! ... (Emma enters with Vito. She looks different, enjoying her freedom, at ease, although she is the stranger in this place. Vito is small, thin. He is smoking.)

EMMA

It's wonderful here.

VITO

This is where we come after work. How many plans have been made here! How many revolutions have been won here!

FEDYA

(At a table with Anna Minkin—she is smoking.) How much beer has been drunk here! (They laugh.) Sit down, Vito. Who is your friend? (Emma and Vito sit.)

VITO

(Calls out to Sachs) Mr. Sachs, two beers! ... This is Emma Goldman. She's just come from Rochester.

FEDYA

And before that?

EMMA

From Kovno, in Russia.

FEDYA

Ah … Kovno.

ANNA

He has no idea where it is. If you said Schmetrogorsk, Fedya would say: "Ah, Schmetrogorsk!"

FEDYA

So, you're from Rochester. I hear it's called the city of flowers.

EMMA

No, the city of flour, like in bread.

FEDYA

Welcome to New York, the city of sewers.

VITO

Fedya can't forget that I work in the sewers.

ANNA

Vito, you work in the sewers. But you're really a philosopher.

VITO

Is there a difference? But it's true. Everyone here is really something else. Anna works in a corset factory, but what is she really? An organizer of the corset workers. Fedya is unemployed. But what is he really? An artist.

FEDYA

Really, I'm unemployed.

EMMA

How is it, to work in the sewers?

VITO

First of all, it's temporary work. Just until there's a general constipation in New York. (Anna shakes her head—she knows Vito.) According to the Marxian theory of capitalist crisis, the rich will get more and more constipated, and the poor will have less and less to eat, so the sewers will run dry. At which point I and my fellow sewer workers, the true proletariat, will rise up (he gets up dramatically), out of the *drek* ...

SACHS

Enough! People are eating ...

VITO

There's no more to say. When that day comes, then you'll see something, Mr. Sachs.

SACHS

When you start paying for beer, then we'll see something.

VITO

Don't worry, I get paid next Friday.

SACHS

My family has to eat Monday, Tuesday, Wednesday, Thursday ... (He holds up fingers.)

VITO

And I don't have to eat?

SACHS

No, you're a revolutionary. You can live on hot air. (Everyone laughs. Sachs resumes his game of *Morra* with the pianist.) *Cinque! Nove! ...*

FEDYA

Laugh! When the revolution comes, we'll collectivize this place, and then we'll have ...

ANNA

Free beer! (Everyone chants: "Free beer! Free beer!" Sachs goes off, shaking his head.)

EMMA

(To Vito, smiling) So, this is how anarchists in New York plan the revolution.?

VITO

We work hard all day, and in the evening ...

ANNA

Yes, during the day, in the shop, we denounce the capitalists. And in the evening, at Sachs' Cafe, we denounce one another. There are the Marxists, and the Bakuninists, and the Kropotkinists, and the DeLeonists ...

EMMA

And you?

ANNA

Ah, when I first read Marx! The *Manifesto!* So clear, so glorious! (She gets up on a chair.) Workers of the world, unite! The capitalist system has created enormous wealth, but it has done this out of the misery of human beings. It is a sick system. How does it solve the problem of unemployment? By war and preparations for war. It must give way to a new society, where people share the work and share the wealth and live as human beings should. (Everyone applauds. Anna bows.) But then I read Bakunin. (Vito makes a gesture of disgust.) At first, I hated him for his attacks on Marx. But I was intrigued. The dictatorship of the proletariat, he said, is like the dictatorship of the bourgeoisie. It will not wither away by itself. It will become a tyranny. There can be no workers' state. The state is an evil in itself. We must have no governments, no gods, no masters. (Emma and Fedya applaud.)

VITO

Bakunin is a dreamer, a romantic. Marx is rooted in history, in reality.

FEDYA

Three cheers for Bakunin!

VITO

Four cheers for Marx!

FEDYA

(Holding up fingers in the *Morra* spirit.) Bakunin!

VITO

Marx!

ANNA

(Laughing) Kropotkin!

VITO

Engels!

SACHS

(Giving them all the finger) The revolution! (A man comes into the cafe. Black hair, spectacles, strong face and jaw. He looks around, is clearly at home here.)

VITO

Hello, Sasha! (Fedya and Anna, too: "Hello, Sasha." Sasha nods, sits down at a nearby table. Vito turns to Emma.) His name is Alexander Berkman. He never speaks until he eats.

SASHA

(Calls to Sachs) Mr. Sachs. A steak, large. And a beer, large.

FEDYA

Sasha, who died and left you money?

SASHA

Today was payday.

VITO

(To Emma) He works in a cigar factory. Guess his age.

EMMA

Thirty-five?

VITO

Twenty-one.

EMMA

He's no older than me.

VITO

Sasha is older than everyone. (He calls over) Hey, Sasha, say hello to our new comrade from Rochester, Emma Goldman.

SASHA

(Looks up, nods, continuing to eat …) Johann Most is speaking at the Academy of Music tomorrow night. (He reaches into his package of rolled-up newspaper.) I have the leaflets here.

EMMA

Johann Most himself?

SASHA

(Looking up at her really for the first time) You've never heard him speak?

EMMA

No, but I read his articles in *Freiheit.*

SASHA

(Nods, continuing to eat, looks up.) Who will distribute on the West Side?

VITO

(To Emma) Sasha doesn't waste a moment. (To Sasha) Okay. I'll do the West Side on my lunch hour. (Sasha hands him a bunch of leaflets.)

ANNA

I'll do Union Square, right after work.

FEDYA

I'll help you. I'll see you there at six.

SASHA.

I've got a shop meeting at lunch time. I'll distribute down on Broome Street an hour before I go to work.

ANNA

Sasha! You'll have to get up before five ...

SASHA

So?

ANNA

So nothing. After the revolution, we will erect a statue right on Broome Street. (She strikes a pose.) Sasha—distributing leaflets before dawn.

EMMA

I have a room right near Broome Street. I'll help you.

SASHA

At five in the morning?

EMMA

If you'll be there, I'll be there.

VITO

Distributing fliers with Sasha is an experience. (He takes a bunch of leaflets, stands up, goes into his act, imitating Sasha on a street corner, speaking with gravity, as if addressing a passerby.) My good friend, do you realize that Johann Most is speaking tonight? Here is the information. (Vito hands the leaflet to Fedya, then switches to the voice of the passerby.) Who? What? I have no time. (Then back to Sasha's voice, with indignation) You have no time! Ten hours a day you give to the capitalists, and you can't spare one hour for the movement that will end your slavery? Shame on you! (He rams the leaflet into Fedya's stomach. Fedya gasps. Everyone laughs. Sasha shakes his head, manages a smile. He can take it. Vito switches.) Fedya distributing leaflets, that's another story. (He assumes a gracious stance.) My dear Madam. I have something for you. Do not fear. It is a free ticket to a concert. A concert of words. A symphony of ideas. The conductor? Johann Most. My pleasure, Madam. (He hands the leaflet to Emma, dances gracefully around her, humming a tune.)

SASHA

Now let's be serious.

VITO

I'm serious, I'm serious. (He pokes another leaflet into Fedya's stomach.)

SASHA

I think it's not correct for Fedya and Anna to go to the same place and me and our friend Goldman to be at the same place. A waste of people. We could be covering more territory.

EMMA

No, it's not a waste. If a policeman comes along, it's harder for him to arrest two at once.

ANNA

She's right.

EMMA

Besides, it looks better to have two people. It shows we are in an organization.

ANNA

She's right.

SASHA

(Annoyed) She's *not* right. She's just come from Rochester, and she's telling us how to distribute leaflets in New York.

EMMA

(Quietly) What a petty display of provincialism.

SASHA

(Aggressively) What was that word?

EMMA

Petty.

SASHA

I mean the other word.

EMMA

Provincialism?

SASHA

I don't know that word. (There is an embarrassed silence.)

EMMA

(Softly) You call yourself an anarchist?

SASHA

(Angrily) Yes!

EMMA

And an internationalist?

SASHA

Of course!

EMMA

Provincialism is the opposite of internationalism.

SASHA

That's an insult!

ANNA

She's right, Sasha.

SASHA

She's right, she's right! Enough already!

VITO

Sasha, it's time you lost an argument.

EMMA

I'll meet you at five, Sasha. On Broome Street. Where the street car stops. (She holds out her hand. Sasha looks at her curiously, slowly extends his hand. They shake hands, looking at one another, the first trace of a smile in Sasha's eyes.)

SCENE 4: MOST SPEAKS

A revolutionary song, taped. The Deutschverein Hall, a spotlight on Johann Most, center stage, coat and tie, crewcut hair, black-grey beard, tall, a distortion on the left side of his face from a childhood accident. He has force and dignity. He was a member of the German Reichstag. He has been imprisoned. He is a veteran of the revolutionary movement. A dramatic speaker, but able to slow down and almost whisper for effect. Here he is giving the audience a lesson in anarchism, as he is giving the police such a lesson. There is a policeman on each side of the stage, holding a club, in semi-darkness. It's a long speech for the stage, and can only work if Most grips the audience.

MOST

Comrades! Friends! And members of the New York City police. (Laughter. Most peers into the audience, using his hand to shade his eyes. He points.) Ah, there is Inspector Sullivan in the fourth row, taking notes. (Laughter, applause.) Please, Inspector, get my name right—it's *Johann Most.* (Most extends his hands, palms up. There is no longer a smile on his face. His tone is changing.) My friends, here we are, at a peaceful meeting. There are women and children in the audience. (There is now anger in his voice.) Yet the walls are lined with police, carrying clubs, armed with guns. Is this what is meant in America by freedom of speech? (Murmurs in the audience.)

Members of the police force, why are you here? Perhaps you have heard that this is a meeting of anarchists. (Laughter) *Yes, we are anarchists!* (Applause.) Perhaps you have heard that we believe in disorder. (He claps his hands sharply together, like a schoolmaster.) Wrong! We believe in *order.* No, not an artificial order, enforced by the club and the gun, the courts and the prisons, but the natural order of human beings living and working together in equality, in harmony. Who says we believe in chaos and disorder? The capitalists and warmakers, the promoters of economic chaos, the architects of world disorder!

(His voice softens.) Let me explain to you, Inspector Sullivan, and to you, members of the police force, how we came to be anarchists. (He pauses, stands very erect.) First, we examined our own lives and found we were living by rules we had not made, in ways we did not want, estranged from our most powerful human desires. Then we opened our eyes and looked around the city. At five in the morning, we could see the workers open their windows to catch a breath of fresh air before going to the factory. In the winter, we saw the corpses of old men and women who froze because they had no fuel. In the summer, we saw the babies in the tenements dying of cholera. (There is total silence.)

(His voice rises. His pace steps up.) And we saw something else. We saw that seven hundred buildings in this city are owned by one family, the Astors, whose fortune is one-hundred-million dollars. We saw that Jay Gould has five hundred acres on the Hudson and a mansion on Fifth Avenue, and that Rockefeller had taken control of the nation's oil. Yes, we saw the rich living from the wealth created by generations of workers. We saw that a party was given at the Waldorf Astoria in honor of a dog. Yes, a dog! Who was dressed in jewels, while mothers on Cherry Street had no milk for their children. (His voice is choked with anger. He waits to get control and speaks more quietly.)

We also saw that these same men who own the industries of America pick the presidents, and the congressmen. They appoint the judges, anoint the priests, own the newspapers, endow the universities. (The police start smacking their clubs in their hands in unison. Most's voice rises above the sound.)

Every year, thirty-five-thousand workers die in *their* mines and mills. Every generation, the sons of the workers are slaughtered in *their* wars. And they accuse us of violence! (He pauses, speaks very deliberately.) Let us make our position clear. Violence against innocent people? Never. Violence against the oppressor? Always! (Applause.) Yes, take notes, Inspector Sullivan. We expect to hear from you. (Laughter.) But we are taking notes, too. And some day, *some day,* you will hear from us!

He bows, to signify the end of the speech, walks off to great applause, the stamping of feet, then the singing of "The Internationale" in German. The police are still smacking their clubs in their palms.

Emma and Anna appear, as those sounds are still heard. They have been in the audience.

ANNA

What a meeting!

EMMA

So that is Johann Most. I know now why he is in and out of prison.

SASHA

(Joining them.) Hello, Anna ... hello, Emma. (Fedya joins them, too. He is wearing a finely embroidered shirt. Sasha shakes his head.) Look at the shirt. You can always tell an artist.

FEDYA

Sasha is annoyed by my shirt.

EMMA

I think it's beautiful.

SASHA

We all have our tastes. But should we spend money on such things when the movement needs every cent we have?

EMMA

Don't we need beautiful things to remind us of what life can be like some day?

SASHA

Should an anarchist enjoy luxuries while people live in poverty?

ANNA

When Jews talk, everyone asks questions. No one gives answers.

EMMA

Must we give up music and the smell of lilacs to be revolutionaries?

ANNA

(Nudging Fedya) See?

SASHA

Who said you have to give up music or flowers? But shirts like
this, yes.

FEDYA

What about art?

SASHA

It's an objective fact: the artist lives on the backs of the poor.
Don't take it personally, Fedya.

FEDYA

Why shouldn't I? Am I not a person?

EMMA

Sasha, there is something wrong with the way you think. I
can't quite express it ...

SASHA

If you were right, you would be able to express it.

EMMA

(Calmly) You are insufferable.

SASHA

(Good-humoredly) I don't know what that means, but I think I have been insulted again.

ANNA

I think, Sasha, it means you want us all to suffer until the revolution comes.

SASHA

You don't understand.

ANNA

I understand, and I'm going home right now—to suffer! Are you coming, Emma?

EMMA

I'll come a little later. I want to change the dates on these posters. Most is speaking again in two weeks.

ANNA

(To the men) She's staying with me until she finds a job. (She starts to leave, nudging Fedya until he begins to comprehend.)

FEDYA

(Simulating a yawn) I'm tired. I'll walk home with you, Anna. (They go off.)

SASHA

(Watching Fedya leave, shaking his head.) He's tired! He sleeps all morning. (He hesitates, his voice softens as he turns to Emma.) How about a little walk?

EMMA

I'm not finished with these posters yet.

SASHA

And let's not argue. After all, we're comrades.

EMMA

Shouldn't comrades argue?

SASHA

Now she wants to argue about arguing! (They are silent as she continues to work on the posters.) Let's go for a seltzer.

EMMA

(Having fun) Isn't that a luxury?

SASHA

(After a pause) A plain seltzer?

EMMA

What if I want a little chocolate syrup in it?

SASHA

(Entering into the spirit) I'm not as dogmatic as you think. A *little* chocolate syrup.

EMMA

(Her tone changes) How did you come to be as you are, Sasha?

SASHA

You mean insufferable?

EMMA

Yes. No. I mean, your ideas. Our ideas. They tell me you're organizing the cigar workers.

SASHA

In the old country, at the age of thirteen, I was expelled from school for writing an essay.

EMMA

For an essay?

SASHA

The title was considered somewhat tactless. "There Is No God." (They laugh.)

EMMA

At thirteen, I was already working in a factory in St. Petersburg. I did not know words like capitalism, anti-Semitism, the State. But it was all so clear. Who needs the words when you feel it in your bones every day?

SASHA

Didn't you think America would be different?

EMMA

In the factory in Rochester, I could feel no difference. Yes, America had a Constitution. But it meant nothing in the factory.

SASHA

It meant nothing for those executed after Haymarket.

EMMA

So many of us had our eyes opened by Haymarket.

SASHA

I'll never forget the last words of Spies to the jury: "These are my ideas. They constitute a part of myself. I cannot divest myself of them, nor would I if I could … I say, if death is the penalty for proclaiming the truth, call your hangman." (Both are moved at hearing those words again.) I hope I will have such courage when the time comes.

EMMA

(Coming closer, grasping his hands) Sasha! You're too young to talk of dying.

SASHA

One day, the choice will be before us, to bow down, or to risk all. To give our lives if necessary.

EMMA

I am ready to give my life for what I believe in. But I would like to give it over a period of fifty years, not in one heroic moment. The movement needs us to live for it, not to die for it.

SASHA

Perhaps only our grandchildren will be able to live full lives.

EMMA

I don't believe that. We must live ourselves. And beautifully, to show how life can be lived. (In her fervor, she has held onto his hands, come closer to him. They are suddenly conscious of their closeness and break away.)

SASHA

(Hesitates) What are you doing tomorrow?

EMMA

I have to go to the baggage room at Grand Central. I left my sewing machine there.

SASHA

You brought it all the way from Rochester?

EMMA

Yes. I'm tired of working in a corset factory. I'd like to work for myself, maybe set up a cooperative shop. Like Vera in *What Is to Be Done?*

SASHA

Oh, have you read Chernyshevsky?

EMMA

Why are you surprised?

SASHA

Well, you're so young.

EMMA

So are you.

SASHA

But I am a man.

EMMA

(Her anger rising) And I am a woman.

SASHA

You are very sensitive.

EMMA

And *you* are very *insensitive*.

SASHA

(Sighing) Do you think you and I will ever be good friends?

EMMA

(Softly) Aren't we? (A second of silence.) Sasha, let's go for that seltzer some other time. Anna is waiting and she needs her sleep.

SASHA

All right! Tomorrow I'll come with you to Grand Central. I know my way around the city. Afterward, if you like, we can take the El down to the Brooklyn Bridge and walk across. The air is wonderful on the river.

EMMA

(Incredulous) I didn't ask you to come with me! Don't you have to work?

SASHA

(A little abashed) This morning, when I went to work, I made a tactical mistake. I gave some of our leaflets to the workers. The foreman said: "This is your last day." So, I'll come for you tomorrow. (Emma starts to respond. He holds up his hand.) I know where Anna Minkin lives. What time? (She doesn't respond.) What time?

EMMA

Ten o'clock.

SASHA

Good. Before I meet you, I can look for a job.

EMMA

I saw how much you eat. You need a job.

SASHA

Emma … I think you are … insufferable. (He turns to go, then turns back. They both smile. He turns again and goes.)

SCENE 5: ANNA'S APARTMENT

Flute music. Emma and Sasha tiptoe into the apartment. It is dark and quiet. She is wearing a sailor hat.

EMMA

Come in, we can talk a while.

SASHA

Will we wake up Anna?

EMMA

Nothing can wake up Anna. (To prove it, she stamps on the floor, then listens. No reaction.) You see? (They slowly embrace in the dark. Then comes Anna's delayed reaction.)

ANNA

(From the other room, sleepily) For God's sake, a little quiet!

(Emma and Sasha break off to listen. Emma shrugs. It is quiet again. They slowly embrace once more, and kiss, the music still soft in the background as the scene ends.)

SCENE 6: FORMING THE COMMUNE

Lively piano music, exuberant, befitting a scene of four young, attractive, life-loving, dedicated people. Emma and Sasha are sitting in Anna Minkin's apartment, having tea in glasses. Sasha is enjoying it, blowing, cooling, sipping. Anna and Fedya enter.

SASHA

Look, he's wearing that shirt again!

EMMA

(To Sasha, softly) Who's going to tell Anna, you or me?

SASHA

I'll tell her.

ANNA

Tell what?

EMMA

That girl hears everything.

ANNA

Yes, *everything*. (She laughs and bends over to kiss Emma.)

EMMA

Anna dear, Toby Golden is moving out of her place on Forsyth Street. It's five dollars a month. Sasha and I are going to take it.

ANNA

(Teasing) So, you'd rather live with Sasha than with me. A true friend!

EMMA

Anna, you know this place is just big enough for you. With me here, you have no privacy at all.

ANNA

You mean ever since Sasha started coming around. (She dances around provocatively, groaning and sighing.) It's been *oy* and *ah,* and *ooh* and *mmm.* Yes (she embraces Emma), you need a place. I know Toby Golden's place. It's twice as big as this apartment, isn't it?

SASHA

Yes, twice as big.

ANNA

Good! Then there's room for me.

SASHA

Now look, Anna …

ANNA

Do you believe in collectivity or not?

SASHA

Of course, but ...

ANNA

(Orating, imitating Sasha, or someone else) Bourgeois individualism corrupts us all! We must begin the new culture right now, comrades! Share and share alike! Break through the prison of monogamy!

EMMA

Of course she's right, Sasha.

SASHA

(Gloomily) Of course she's right.

FEDYA

(Has been walking around, rearranging pictures on the walls, and now stops.) I know Toby Golden's place. There are three big rooms.

ANNA

Yes, you see?

FEDYA

Yes, it's big enough for me, too.

ANNA

You, too?

FEDYA

(Jumping onto the bed, imitating Anna.) We must begin the new culture now, comrades. Love thy neighbor, says the

Bible. Workers of the world, unite, says Marx. Live in free association, says Kropotkin. Make room for Fedya, says Fedya!

ANNA

Fedya, I'm not the same with you as Emma is with Sasha. We're just friends.

FEDYA

Yes, and we'll live together as friends. What do we always say? (He orates again.) Between men and women there must be an endless variety of relationships—passion, companionship …

ANNA

Hostility! Murder! (She attacks him.)

EMMA

(Excited) The four of us together! It *is* big enough. There's a bedroom, and we can put a bed in the living room, and a folding bed in the kitchen.

SASHA

(He has been gloomy in the corner. Now he is aroused.) Why stop with four? How about a bed in the bathroom, too? Then my friend Yussel Miller can join us. We could put the bed upright and Yussel can sleep standing up. (He is a little bitter.)

EMMA

(Disapprovingly) Sasha!

SASHA

Don't say another word. (He comes over to them, puts his

arms around them.) You are right. You are all right. When I'm wrong, I admit it. We're all friends and comrades. Why can't we live together, live collectively? That's the way of the future. And we have to start the future now. (He doesn't look happy.)

ANNA

(Jumping up) Yes! Yes!

FEDYA

(Producing a bottle of wine he had wrapped in a newspaper) Let's drink to our little collective.

SASHA

(Shaking his head) Every time you see him, he has a bottle of wine.

FEDYA

(Uncorking it with a loud noise right in front of Sasha) Emma, you wash some glasses. I'll pour the wine. (Emma shrugs and goes to do it.)

SASHA

We'll all contribute equally to the rent and food.

EMMA

We'll all contribute according to our ability. Anna and I are working in a corset shop. You're working in a cigar factory.

SASHA

And Fedya can sell his shirt. We can live on that for a month.

ANNA

Don't laugh. When Fedya sells a painting, he makes more than I can make in a week.

SASHA

Fedya, when's the last time you sold a painting?

FEDYA

What day is it?

ANNA

Wednesday.

FEDYA

(Counting on his fingers) About a year ago …

SASHA

Well, I can see we will eat well.

FEDYA

None of us will eat as well as you, Sasha. You eat and drink as much as the three of us.

EMMA

To each according to his need. Sasha needs to eat like a horse. Fedya needs to sleep late in the morning. I need to read without people talking to me. And Anna (she turns her head mischievously), Anna needs to spend about an hour in the toilet every morning.

ANNA

A perfect group! We'll never interfere with one another. Fedya will be sleeping. Sasha will be eating. Emma will be reading. And I'll be in the toilet. (She takes their hands to execute a little place-changing routine.) And every hour, we can change places.

FEDYA

Let's drink to our needs! (Emma pours wine for all of them. Sasha slugs it down with great enjoyment.)

SASHA

We can organize the tenants in Toby's building.

EMMA

Oh, what the four of us can do together! (Fedya pours the wine for all of them. Again Sasha drinks it down in a gulp and Fedya pours him another. Anna starts singing a Yiddish tune—"Mein Greeneh Kuzine." She takes Emma's hand and they dance. Then Emma takes Fedya's hand and the three of them dance.) Come on, Sasha!

SASHA

Each to his need. I'll have more wine. (He pours himself another glass as the others spin around him. But then he starts dancing himself.) To tell you the truth, I think I'm a little drunk! (He's smiling happily, suddenly calls out) Fedya, I want your shirt! (Fedya flamboyantly takes off his shirt, throws it at Sasha. Sasha holds it over his head, dancing. All four dance exuberantly as the music quickens to "Mein Greeneh Kuzine," as the scene ends.)

SCENE SEVEN: FEDYA AND EMMA

Fedya is sketching on the kitchen table. He looks up in surprise. Emma has just come in, weary. She puts down her workbag.

EMMA

It's so hot up here, Fedya. How can you work? It's worse than the shop.

FEDYA

You're home so early. Is something wrong?

EMMA

Kargman found out who is organizing the union. Three of us were fired this morning. It was a big commotion. More girls wanted to walk out, but we told them to wait. After work today, there'll be a meeting, and if enough girls come ... well, we'll see ... Oh God, it's so hot. (She removes her shirt, and is wearing a camisole.)

FEDYA

Emma, what are you doing?

EMMA

(Amused) Fedya, darling, you've seen me like this before.

FEDYA

Yes, with everybody here. But like this ...

EMMA

I'll put my blouse back on, if it makes you nervous.

FEDYA

Why should I be nervous? After all, I'm an artist. At the Settlement House, we painted nude figures all the time. We had models. Now I can't afford that. I paint nudes from memory. (He smiles.) And my memory is not too good.

EMMA

If you ever want me to pose for you Fedya, just tell me.

FEDYA

You're serious, Emma?

EMMA

Why not? We're friends and comrades. (She leans over and kisses him on the cheek. He gets up and paces the floor nervously.) What's the matter?

FEDYA

I would like you to pose for me, Emma. But I don't know ...

EMMA

What is it?

FEDYA

(He stops pacing, comes over to her) I have been so troubled. (Shakes his head.) Sasha is my friend, and yet ... I have been longing for you, Emma. I have, yes. I can't help it ... (He takes her hand. With her other hand, she strokes his hair.)

EMMA

Sweet Fedya. It's all right. It's all right. We both love Sasha. But Sasha and I don't own one another. Why shouldn't you have feelings for me? Why shouldn't I have feelings for you?

FEDYA

(Taking both her hands) Emma ... do you think ...

EMMA

Why are we living? Why are we struggling and organizing? What is this all for? Sometimes, in the midst of all the turmoil, I forget, and I have to remind myself, and then I think of the very first time I realized my life could be ... ecstatic. It was back in the old country. I must have been eight or nine. This peasant boy worked around the farm, and one day he took me out in the meadow. The sun was strong. We sat in the long grass and he played his flute. Then he lifted me in his arms and threw me into the air and caught me. Everything smelled of grass. My soul melted. He caught me again and again. (Fedya presses his lips to her hair.) Years after that, I was with my aunt in Konigsberg. She took me to the opera. *Il Trovatore.* Such golden voices. Such heavenly music. I had never in my life been to any theater—I sat there in the balcony as in a trance. When it was over, I heard the crash of applause. Everyone was leaving, and my aunt was calling me, but I sat there in my seat, the tears streaming down my face ... When we sailed for America, out of my old life, almost everything was forgotten, but on the boat I thought of the peasant boy on the farm and the opera house in Konigsberg. I knew so little, but at that moment I knew what I wanted life to be ... (She throws her arms around

Fedya, and he around her, in a long embrace. He sits up, shakes his head in confusion.)

EMMA

What's the matter?

FEDYA

I am Sasha's friend.

EMMA

That makes it better.

FEDYA

I feel like a betrayer.

EMMA

You've taken nothing from him. He and I are still as we were.

FEDYA

Will he see it that way?

EMMA

You know Sasha. At first he will be angry.

FEDYA

Oh, will he be angry!

EMMA

He may smash a piece of furniture.

FEDYA

Maybe two or three.

EMMA

And then he'll say …

FEDYA

(Orating like Sasha) I was wrong—when I'm wrong, I admit it. We must live like free people—we must live as in the future society.

EMMA

Yes, that's exactly what he will say.

FEDYA

I love Sasha … (Music as scene ends.)

SCENE 8: STRIKE AT KARGMAN'S

Picket line, including Emma and Anna, with signs, walking, shouting. One picket has a bandaged head. A policeman stands by, holding a club.

PICKETS

Strike! Strike! Stay out! Don't work for Kargman, stay out! Strike! Strike! Don't work for Kargman, stay out! (Another striker comes running up to the line, excited …)

STRIKER

Scabs! They're bringing scabs! (A small group of girls, women, led by a well-dressed man, arrive. The striker who just spoke picks up a rock. Emma puts a hand on his arm.)

EMMA

No, Yankele, wait. (The pickets mass in front of the shop entrance. The scabs stop.) Look at them. They're just off the boat. Look at their faces. They're hungry, just like us! (Yankele moves back. The scab leader rushes forward, knocking Emma down. Her friends rush back. The policeman moves in, lifts his club threateningly, they move back to the line. Emma walks back and forth quickly around the scabs, speaking to them.) *Schwester! Bruder! Herr zu!* Listen to me! They didn't tell you there's a strike here, and you are taking our jobs. (The man leading the scabs comes up to her threateningly and grabs her arm.)

MAN

Get the hell away from here before I break your head! (Emma pulls her arm away angrily. The other strikers have come off the line to her side.)

EMMA

Keep walking, comrades! (She keeps walking herself, continuing to speak to the scabs, then stops as someone puts a box before her. She mounts it, at first hesitantly, then lifts her head and addresses the scabs directly, appealingly.) I know you need to work. Your families are hungry. *Azoi wie unsere.* Just like ours! Your houses are cold. *Azoi wie unsere!* Just like ours. Kargman has promised you good wages. But let me tell you something, brothers and sisters. We know Kargman well. He is a liar! *Er iz ah ligner!* But you know that already, because he didn't tell you there was a strike here! He despises you, just as he despises us. *Er iz dein Sonne!* He is your enemy! Just as he is ours. He will pay you good wages, yes, until the strike is over. But what happens then? Then he will cut your wages, as he cut ours. And you'll go on strike, just like us. And the police will come and smash you with their clubs, just as they do to us! And then Kargman will get others to take your place. (The policeman moves toward her, raises his club. She raises her picket stick. He steps back. She continues talking.) Brothers! Sisters! (She is gaining confidence. This is her first speech. The well-dressed man calls to the scabs: "Come on, let's go in!" He starts pushing forward. The scabs seem uncertain. Emma is speaking with great strength now.) *Schwester! Bruder!* (The power and urgency in her voice makes them turn.) If you try to go in, there'll be a fight. We shouldn't fight one another. Together we can make our lives better. Listen. We are not alone! All over the country, working people like us are joining together. Right now, in Pennsylvania, three thousand workers are saying "Enough!" to the richest man in America, Andrew Carnegie. Enough, to working twelve hours a day in the steel furnaces! Enough to a heat like in hell! Enough to fourteen cents an hour! Enough! Three thousand workers standing together, refusing to scab on one another ... Let us stand together, too! Join us, my brothers and sisters. (Almost a whisper now) Don't work for Kargman! (They seem frozen in place by her words. The well-dressed man is shouting at them: "Inside! Inside!" But they don't move. Then one of them, a woman, shawl on her head, comes forward to Emma. She is weeping. She holds out her hands. Emma grasps them. The picket line continues chanting.)

PICKETS

Stay out! Stay out! Don't work for Kargman! Strike! Strike!

SCENE 9: THE DECISION TO KILL FRICK

Opera music from Bizet's Carmen. *Sasha is sitting at the kitchen table, writing intently. Emma comes in from outside, flushed, holding violets, humming from the opera music. She puts an arm around Sasha gaily, kisses him on the cheek.*

EMMA

Oh, what a picket line at Kargman's today!

SASHA

(Without looking up, continuing to write) Anna told me. You made your first speech. She said it was good ... (He looks up.) You've been away all evening.

EMMA

Yes. (She hums ... Sasha does not respond, continues working.) Sasha dear, what are you doing up so late?

SASHA

(Without looking up) A leaflet on the strike in Pittsburgh. Have you heard the latest news?

EMMA

No.

SASHA

Carnegie has put Frick in charge. You know him? Henry Clay Frick. A lover of art. A gangster. And Frick has called in the Pinkertons. You know them? The biggest strike-breaking agency in America. Two thousand men, with the latest weapons.

EMMA

A private army …

SASHA

And Frick is going to use them to break the strike. The strikers will need money, weapons, support from all over the country, or they are done for. I must finish this leaflet tonight. (He looks up at Emma.) Where have you been all evening?

EMMA

Johann invited me to go to the Metropolitan Opera House with him. We saw *Carmen*.

SASHA

Johann? (His temper is rising.) Johann who?

EMMA

Johann Most.

SASHA

So now it's *Johann!* The opera! That's how Most uses the movement's money. (He thinks.) The opera must have ended hours ago.

EMMA

We went to a restaurant afterward.

SASHA

A restaurant! You probably drank wine all evening, too.

EMMA

(Heatedly) Yes, we drank wine!

SASHA

Of course. Most loves expensive wine. That's our great revolutionary leader.

EMMA

Most is a wonderful man. You told me so yourself. He gave up his seat in the German Reichstag. He became an anarchist. He spent years in prison. He risked his life!

SASHA

(Coldly) The movement gives no special benefits for war veterans. The most heroic figures can become corrupt. We see that in history.

EMMA

Then I am corrupt, too, by going to the opera, by drinking wine?

SASHA

Yes! You, too! You're worse than Most, you with your pretensions, cuddling up to every leader in the movement ...

EMMA

Shut your mouth!

SASHA

I'm speaking the truth, and you know it. What are you holding there?

EMMA

(Defiantly) They're violets. Yes, I know flowers are an unnecessary expense when people are starving. Well, they are beautiful, and I love them. (She goes to put them in a jar.)

SASHA

It makes me nauseous to see them when the strikers in Pittsburgh are in need of bread.

EMMA

(Angered and hurt) And what are *you* doing about the families in Pittsburgh? Writing a leaflet!

SASHA

Yes, we need to write leaflets.

EMMA

It will take more than that.

SASHA

(Shouting) And I'm prepared to do more than that.

EMMA

So am I. And so is Most.

SASHA

We will see.

EMMA

What do you mean?

SASHA

We will see.

EMMA

(More softly) Don't you understand, Sasha? We can't all live at the level of the most oppressed. We have to have a little beauty in our lives, even in the midst of struggle.

SASHA

You think Most cares about beauty? What you think was in Most's mind when he gave you those violets?

EMMA

You're jealous, Sasha. I thought you had overcome that. I thought you believed in my freedom.

SASHA

Freedom, yes! Decadence, no! With Fedya it is different. Fedya, we both love. But Most! He is not good for you, Emma.

EMMA

(Angrily) Who is to decide that, you or me?

SASHA

(A little subdued) Yes, that's for you to decide. (He is suddenly angry at her scoring a point, and he bangs his fist on the table.)

ANNA

(Emerging from her room in her nightgown) Will you two stop that? You've kept me up for the past half-hour. I've got to be on the picket line early in the morning. You do, too, Emma. (Another voice from the next apartment: "Shut up in there!" Some banging on the walls, general protest over loss of sleep. Someone yells: "Quiet already!")

EMMA

Yes, for God's sake, let's go to sleep.

ANNA

(Turning on her) You don't care. None of you care any more—you and Sasha and Fedya—you're moving to Wor-chester, Massachusetts, so you don't give a damn about anybody.

EMMA

(Correcting her) *Wooster.*

ANNA

(Rejecting the correction) To Wor-chester. And without me.

EMMA

You said you wanted to have nothing to do with our idea.

ANNA

Such a brilliant idea. An ice cream parlor run by revolutionaries. What kind of revolution will you have today, sir? Vanilla? Chocolate? Not strawberry! Not a real, *red* revolution. Not in a petty-bourgeois ice cream parlor!

EMMA

It's just for a little while, Anna. We need the money to start our new magazine.

ANNA

The three of you are leaving me here alone. (Her voice is breaking.)

SASHA

You wanted to stay, Anna.

ANNA

I didn't want to go to Wor-chester. (She bursts out crying. Emma comforts her.)

EMMA

(Wearily) Why are we all fighting? Let's go to sleep. (Voices from other apartment, shouting: "Go to sleep, you bums!")

SASHA

(Replying to the voices) Go to hell, all of you!

ANNA

You wanted to organize them, now you curse them.

SASHA

Oh, shut up and go back to sleep.

ANNA

(To Emma) How can you put up with that man? (She starts to leave. Fedya arrives.)

FEDYA

What's all this noise?

EMMA

Go to sleep!

FEDYA

I'll go to sleep when I feel like! (He returns now to his usual low-key demeanor.) Did you hear about Pittsburgh? (Anna turns back to listen.)

EMMA

Sasha told me. The Pinkertons have been called in.

FEDYA

Well, they started. There was a battle there today.

SASHA

Today?

FEDYA

Frick brought three hundred Pinkertons down the river on a barge. An army of them. Machine guns, rifles. They opened fire on men, women, children. There are seven dead. (Emma puts her hands to her head as if to shut out the news.)

SASHA

(Looking at Emma, with combined anguish and fury) While you were at the opera! (He smashes the vase of violets with a sweep of his hand.)

EMMA

(Shouting, weeping) While you were writing a damn leaflet! Don't talk to me that way, you bastard!

FEDYA

Stop it, you two. What are we going to do?

SASHA

(To himself, pacing the floor, fists clenched) What's wrong with me? I must be crazy! Going with you two to Massachusetts to open an ice cream parlor so we can publish some intellectual garbage! I must be out of my mind. I should be in Pittsburgh right now, with the strikers.

EMMA

And what are you going to do in Pittsburgh?

SASHA

It was you who said: "It will take more than leaflets ..."

EMMA

Yes, I said it, but ...

SASHA

But! But! There is something that must be done in Pittsburgh. (He is speaking calmly, thoughtfully now. The others watch him as he paces the floor, building up his rationale and his resolve at the same time.) We must show the world that the Carnegies, the Rockefellers, the Fricks are not invincible. We see their pictures in the newspapers. The arrogance in their faces. The contempt in their eyes for all who have not succeeded in their game of becoming rich. Yes, the pictures. Frick going to church. Frick in the White House with the President, while his workers fall from exhaustion in the mills. Frick drinking whiskey at his country club while his detectives shoot down women and children. Frick. Frick. Yes, there is something that must be done in Pittsburgh.

FEDYA

What are you talking about?

SASHA

Frick must die.

EMMA

Keep your voice down. Are you crazy?

SASHA

What does your friend Most say? "There are times in history when a bullet speaks louder than a thousand manifestos."

EMMA

Yes. Yes. (She is thinking desperately, not sure of what to do, and speaks almost to herself.) We have all said to one another that when the right time came ...

FEDYA

(Excited) We would be ready! Yes, we said that. We all did. (There is anguish in his voice now as it all becomes more real.)

SASHA

I'm going to Pittsburgh ...

EMMA

We'll all go. It is the right moment. All through the centuries they have slaughtered the working people. They are never punished. And now once more. But this time, it will be different. We will show everyone—they can die, too!

ANNA

(Trembling) The four of us can do it.

FEDYA

It will have to be planned very carefully. (He is nervous.)

EMMA

But it will go around the world. It is the right time. We can do it.

SASHA

(Quietly) Who kills Frick surrenders his life.

EMMA

(Crying out) We said we are ready. Remember how the four of us said we are ready? How we would stand together when the time came?

SASHA

I will do it alone. (A second of silence, astonishment.)

EMMA

You are crazy, Sasha!

SASHA

No, we will not give them four lives for one. No.

EMMA

You're not going to do it by yourself!

FEDYA

What are we talking about? It takes money to go to Pittsburgh. And what will it be? A bomb? A gun? It takes money.

SASHA

That's right. And we don't have the train fare for one.

EMMA

If we can raise the money for one, we can do it for four. I will get the money somehow.

SASHA

(Shaking his head slowly, firmly) It's not the money.

EMMA

(Almost screaming, but trying to keep her voice down) Well, what is it then? You want to do it all by yourself? You want to say to hell with our comradeship, our love? Is that it?

SASHA

You don't understand. If Frick is killed, someone must explain. Someone must know why it was done, and explain. Otherwise they will say, as they always do, it was the work of a madman.

FEDYA

They will say it anyway.

SASHA

No, Emma can explain it. She has the tongue. She has the gift. She can do it. All of you must stay behind and make it clear to the whole country, to the world.

FEDYA

(Almost in tears) But I'm not needed for that. I'm no speaker.
I can help you, Sasha. Together …

SASHA

(Shouting) No! (The word comes like an explosion.) Fedya,
we don't have to sacrifice you, too.

EMMA

Keep your voices down. (She is in despair.)

SASHA

You know I'm right. You know it's necessary. A moment comes when someone must act, must point, must say:
"Enough!" You know that …

EMMA

(Almost whispering) Yes, Sasha …

SASHA

(Very calm now) All right … money. A train ticket. A device
that will kill …

EMMA

(Becoming calm now, holding back her feelings) You will
need a new suit of clothes …

ANNA

(Almost in tears) Yes …

SASHA

(Totally calm) Let's sit down and make plans. (With a sudden gesture he embraces Fedya, Anna, Emma. They hold him tightly. Then, almost in slow motion, they sit down at the table as the lights go down to end the scene.)

SCENE 10: THE ATTEMPT

In the darkness, a steady beat. Then an eerie light on the scene, which will take place in semi-darkness. Frick and another man are sitting, talking, on one side of the stage, while Sasha can be seen on the other side, in the shadows, getting dressed in his new suit.

MAN

Is that the American way, to riot in the street when things don't go right?

FRICK

We don't riot when things don't go right. We go through the proper channels.

MAN

We go to the Speaker of the House.

FRICK

We go to the Attorney General.

MAN

We go to the Secretary of the Treasury.

FRICK

And they always respond to us with generosity.

MAN

That is democracy ... (Sasha stands up, fully dressed, faces the Frick office.)

SECRETARY'S VOICE

Do you have an appointment? Mr. Frick cannot see you now. You must see Miss O'Neil.

MISS O'NEIL'S VOICE

I'm sorry, but Mr. Frick cannot see you now. (Her voice rises) Where are you going?

SASHA

(Walking toward Frick, calls out) Frick! (Frick rises. Sasha fires, misses. Pandemonium. Sasha is pounced upon by two men who have run into the office. He breaks loose, goes at Frick with a knife, stabs, is knocked down, bodies over him. You see an arm with a hammer rising and falling. Sasha is groaning. Then silence, darkness. Then Sasha's voice, weak, delirious with pain, almost a whisper) My glasses! Where are my glasses? I can't see ... I can't see ...

End of Act One

ACT TWO

PROLOGUE: THE SENTENCING

TAPED VOICE

Alexander Berkman, for the attempted murder of Henry Clay Frick, you are sentenced to the Western Pennsylvania State Penitentiary for a period of twenty-two years. (Rapping of a gavel.)

EMMA

(Standing in the shadows, as if watching the scene from five-hundred miles away, cries out in anguish) Sa-sha-a-a!

SCENE 1: JOHANN MOST SPEAKS

Lights up on Johann Most, center stage, hand extended toward the audience. The beat of a revolutionary song in the background, in German.

MOST

Comrades, some here are circulating petitions for Alexander Berkman. I have refused to sign. Let me explain: revolutionary violence is one thing—a comic opera is another. (Applause. Most holds up his hand. He is serious. His humor is biting. He doesn't mind if people laugh, but his intent is serious. He doesn't smile.) Comrades! I am not urging anyone here to assassinate the nearest capitalist—well, not publicly. (Laughter and applause.) But let me say this: if you decide on it, please do it efficiently. (Laughter.) They tell me that before the shooting, Berkman made a bomb to kill Frick. There was only one thing wrong with Berkman's bomb—it would not explode! (More laughter.) Now comrades, I'm not urging the making of bombs—no never! (He is ironic—everyone knows he *has* urged making bombs.) But it seems to me there is one essential requirement for a bomb. It should explode! I understand Berkman's trade is cigar-making. Maybe he thought it was like making a cigar. (Laughter.) Well, all right, his cigar—I mean, his bomb—did not work. So he fired his gun. Comrades, one piece of advice: if you fire a gun at a capitalist, don't close your eyes! (Laughter, applause.) When his shots missed, he took out his knife. Now we must admire one thing about Berkman—he was well-armed! (More laughter.) But what he really needed was a guillotine, and an agreement from Frick to hold his head still ... (A woman has stood up in the audience, not immediately recognizable, because she is in the front row, facing Most, or on the aisle.) Comrades (getting serious now, emphasizing each word), *we have a revolution to make, and we will have to do it right!* So don't come to me (showing anger) with petitions for that fool, Alexander Berkman! (Applause. The woman is still standing. Most peers into the audience to see who it is. Then, graciously ...) Comrades, I recognize Emma Goldman, who is known to you as an organizer of the cloak and suit workers. I believe she has a question ...

EMMA

(Her voice strong and clear) I have no question. (She just stands there.)

MOST

(Trying to maintain the appearance of good humor) No question?

EMMA

(Loudly) Shame on you, Johann Most!

MOST

(Straining for humor) That is not a question ...

EMMA

(Her voice shaking with anger) Shame, shame on you! (She leaps onto the stage and stands facing Most. He is angry, rattled.)

MOST

Do you have a question?

EMMA

(She is dressed in a long cloak. She pulls a whip from under her cloak and as she strikes Most with it, she cries out ...) Shame! (Most falls back, covers his face. Four strokes more with the whip.) Shame! Shame! Shame! Shame! (Several men jump on stage to stop her. She flings the whip at Most, then turns to the audience, standing straight, and says, in a low emotional voice …) Shame on all of you!

SCENE 2: EMMA MEETS BEN REITMAN

Ragtime music. Fedya and Emma on a station platform. She is carrying a suitcase, wearing a hat, looking quite respectable.

EMMA

How good of you to wait with me, Fedya dear. I know how busy you are these days with your art.

FEDYA

A lucky chance that I have an exhibition in the same city where you are giving a lecture. It's been so long since …

EMMA

Yes. (She grasps his hand.)

FEDYA

Who is meeting you?

EMMA

A Dr. Reitman. I don't know anything about him. (A man has been standing on the opposite side of the stage. Dark hair falling over his eyes. Tall, with a mustache, wearing a silk tie and a big hat, carrying a cane. A confident man.)

EMMA

(Glancing over, amused) Is that how men dress in Chicago?

FEDYA

A bit odd. But handsome, no?

EMMA

Handsome, yes. But a bit odd.

FEDYA

(Whispering ... the man is walking towards them.) I think ...

REITMAN

Miss Emma Goldman?

EMMA

Yes ...

REITMAN

(Grandly) Welcome to Chicago. An honor indeed, Miss Goldman. I am Dr. Ben Reitman. (He bows with a flourish. Emma and Fedya exchange glances.)

EMMA

This is my friend Fedya.

REITMAN

A friend of Emma Goldman is a person to be cherished. (His speech, his manner, are florid, grandiose.)

FEDYA

(Amused) Well, Emma, I leave you in good hands. (They embrace. He goes off.)

EMMA

You are taking me to the Workers' Hall?

REITMAN

No, the chief of police has closed it in anticipation of your arrival.

EMMA

Well, of course … (She is sardonic.)

REITMAN

So this morning I was asked if I would allow the use of my headquarters for your lecture.

EMMA

Your headquarters?

REITMAN

Yes, it's called Hobo Hall.

EMMA

I was told you are a doctor.

REITMAN

Indeed, I am. But my work is among the city's outcasts. I have a storefront in which they stay, and my people are now setting up two-hundred-and-fifty chairs. I assure you, they will be filled. I have spent most of the day with them putting up placards all over the city.

EMMA

Your people? Bums, tramps, hobos, pimps, prostitutes, petty criminals—people so destitute that both bourgeoisie and revolutionists scorn them. You are berating me and the anarchist movement. But how did they become *your* people?

REITMAN

I am an outcast myself. At the age of eleven, I was on my own. I wandered the earth: work gangs in Mexico, the San Francisco earthquake, to Europe on a tramp steamer.

EMMA

How did you get to medical school?

REITMAN

In Chicago, I found a job in the laboratory at the College of Physicians and Surgeons. One day, a famous doctor didn't show up to give his lecture. I had heard him lecture before. I put on a white coat and delivered his lecture as I remembered it.

EMMA

The school officials must have been outraged.

REITMAN

They were. But they gave me a scholarship.

EMMA

And so you became a doctor?

REITMAN

Yes, but I refuse to sell my knowledge for money. I give it to people in need. And they give me what I need.

EMMA

Affection? Devotion? Love?

REITMAN

You understand me, and I understand you.

EMMA

Really?

REITMAN

Yes. That's why I was happy to help with your lecture tonight.

EMMA

The police may close your place, too.

REITMAN

I am on good terms with the police.

EMMA

Then you cannot be on good terms with me.

REITMAN

We have found, by diligent search, a difference between us. I believe in speaking to everyone. Including the police.

EMMA

Surely you know what the police do—to *your* people.

REITMAN

I know very well. Don't you think I have been arrested? Just last week, in the march of the unemployed here in Chicago. They knocked me around a bit in the station house.

EMMA

And you still …

REITMAN

The police are no different than the prostitutes and thieves I work with every day—deprived people, acting out of desperation.

EMMA

There is truth in what you say. And also great innocence.

REITMAN

I believe I can make friends with any human being.

EMMA

You have supreme confidence in yourself.

REITMAN

I know what I can do. Just as you know what you can do. (He takes her arm. She withdraws it.)

EMMA

I know I can walk very well without support.

REITMAN

My object is not support.

EMMA

No?

REITMAN

No. It is to hold the arm of a woman I have admired for years.

                                    EMMA

You don't know me.

                                    REITMAN

I know your ideas. I know what you think about government,
about prisons, about men and women.

                                    EMMA

So you know all about me?

                                    REITMAN

No, not all. One thing I am curious about.

                                    EMMA

Only one thing?

                                    REITMAN

Yes.

                                    EMMA

What is that?

                                    REITMAN

(Quietly) I wonder if your breasts are as beautiful as I imagine
them.

                                    EMMA

(Stepping away from him and looking directly into his face)
Are you crazy?

                                    REITMAN

Is it crazy to be honest?

EMMA

(Laughing) Do you know what I am speaking about tonight?

REITMAN

No.

EMMA

About arrogant men who think they have but to touch a woman's arm to produce an orgasm of delight. And about women who are stupid enough, slavish enough, to accept that. (Her laughter has turned to anger.)

REITMAN

Then your speech is not about me. And not about you. (Emma looks at him intently.) Ah, here we are. (They have been, presumably, walking towards Hobo Hall—he stops at the door.) Can we meet after your lecture?

EMMA

I don't think so.

REITMAN

We could share some wine, talk.

EMMA

Women like me don't trust men like you.

REITMAN

There are no men like me. And no women like you.

EMMA

(Deliberately) *I* don't trust *you.* (She reaches for the door, opens it decisively, and walks through. Reitman follows, turns to face the audience, to introduce her.)

REITMAN

(Bowing grandly) My friends, here is the woman we have all been waiting to hear, America's High Priestess of Anarchism, Miss Emma Goldman. (Great applause. Emma comes forward to face the audience.)

EMMA

I am glad to see so many women in the audience. But tonight, my friends, I speak of the tragedy of women's emancipation. Why tragedy? Because what is now called emancipation is a delusion. There is this idea that women will be emancipated by the vote. But has the vote emancipated men? There is this idea that women will be emancipated by leaving the home and going to work. Has work emancipated men? This tragically emancipated woman is afraid to drink of the fountain of life. She is afraid of ecstasy, and so afraid of men. She will no longer be afraid of men when she learns that her freedom must come from and through herself. She must say: "I am a personality, not a commodity." She must say: "I refuse anyone's right over my body. I will have children or not have them as I wish. I will refuse to be a servant to God, to the State, to a husband. I will make my life simpler, deeper, richer." Such a woman will be afire with freedom, and she will light up the world for everyone! (Applause, cheers, lights down, then up again on Emma and Reitman walking toward a table.)

REITMAN

I come here often. It's a quiet place. You should have some food. (He holds her chair as she sits, and then he sits.)

EMMA

(Shaking her head) After a lecture, I can't eat. Some wine perhaps.

REITMAN

(Calling out) Waiter, a bottle of Bordeaux. (Then, to Emma) Your lecture tonight was magnificent.

EMMA

You are a good organizer. The hall was full, despite the police.

REITMAN

I know what attracts people. I am not shy about doing what is necessary for the causes I believe in. Once I stood in downtown Chicago with an open umbrella—but all that was left of the umbrella was the metal skeleton. It wasn't raining. People would stop and ask me why I held this strange umbrella. I would reply, "Is it more absurd than the system we live in, which gives you something to hold on to, a framework pretending to give protection, and results in your being drenched every time there is a downpour?"

EMMA

(Laughing) That *is* clever.

REITMAN

More than clever. It is true. And everyone who lives in this world knows it to be true, and is just waiting for someone to say it. (He pauses.) Who manages your speaking tours?

EMMA

No one.

REITMAN

If I were your manager, I would double your audiences. No, triple them.

EMMA

I know very little about you or even your ideas. I think you are Jewish. But you wear a cross. I think you are a political agitator, but you get along with the police.

REITMAN

I am a Jew by ancestry, a Baptist by choice, a socialist by conviction, a friend of policemen by practical need, and an anarchist by instinct. If I managed your lectures, we would sell anarchist literature and raise money for the movement beyond anything you can imagine.

EMMA

I *was* surprised at the size of the crowd tonight.

REITMAN

I appealed to their curiosity. Many had not heard of you. I put up posters: this is Emma Goldman, the anarchist; this is Emma Goldman, the apostle of free love. And they were not disappointed tonight. Nor was I. What you said—so true.

Emancipated women, afraid of love, of passion. I know that you have no such fear.

EMMA

(Amused) By what I said?

REITMAN

By your eyes. Those extraordinary blue eyes.

EMMA

Those eyes are tired.

REITMAN

It's been a long day for you. You have a place to stay?

EMMA

I have friends in Chicago.

REITMAN

Can I count myself as one of them?

EMMA

As you like.

REITMAN

Is it a matter of indifference to you?

EMMA

I don't know yet (sipping her wine, smiling).

REITMAN

How will you find out?

EMMA

Life will unfold and I will know.

REITMAN

Let us help it unfold.

EMMA

What do you mean?

REITMAN

Stay with me tonight.

EMMA

You are remarkable! We know one another for three hours.

REITMAN

You spoke tonight of passion. That has no thought of time.

EMMA

I also spoke of a woman being made into a sex commodity.

REITMAN

Of course. But a woman like you? Never. No man would dare. Do you know what courage it takes to approach you? Do you know how I am trembling inside? Feel my hand. (She looks at him directly, hesitates, takes his hand. They look at one another silently—he speaks more softly.) I promise you … a marvelous night.

EMMA

(Laughing) Such modesty! (She drops his hand. He touches her cheek gently and looks into her eyes.) I am very tired, Dr. Reitman.

REITMAN

Call me Ben. But I *am* a doctor. (He holds up his hands.) See these hands? I want to soothe your body tonight, awaken it. It will give me great pleasure. It will give you great pleasure. It will be a rare moment in history!

EMMA

You are a little crazy! (Pauses) But I do like you. (She looks at him intently, then slowly lifts her hand to stroke his hair very gently as the lights go down.)

SCENE 3: PLAN FOR ESCAPE

Reprise music, "Mein Ruhe Platz," signaling the old group. Vito, Anna, Fedya, sitting at a table in Vito's flat, drinking tea.

FEDYA

A good idea, Anna, to bring us together again.

ANNA

It was Emma's idea. But she's not here yet.

FEDYA

(Looking around) You have a nice place here, Vito. How long has it been, my friends?

ANNA

Since Sasha was taken from us? Nine years.

FEDYA

Yes, a nice place, Vito. (He lifts his head.) But what is that smell?

VITO

(Pointing to the window) You see down there? It's a stable.

ANNA

I love horses.

VITO

It's an elephant stable.

FEDYA

Even better.

VITO

Believe me, it lowers the rent.

FEDYA

And good for the lungs. (He holds his nose.)

VITO

It's true. After a day in the sewer, I come home, open the window, and take a deep breath. What a pleasure! (He goes to the window, breathes deeply, then closes the window and grasps his chest in mock pain.)

ANNA

Vito, will you ever grow up?

FEDYA

Let us hope not. Who knows what he will grow into?

ANNA

Where is Emma? She should have been here an hour ago.

VITO

You know where she is. She's with Reitman. (The others are silent—they would rather not comment, but Vito is working himself up.) How can she stay with that faker?

FEDYA

It's not hard to understand. Reitman is a charmer. And he worships her. He works hard, organizes her lecture tours, goes everywhere with her. He is her serf.

VITO

And she is his slave. She seems to be—obsessed. What is there about him, Anna? Maybe you can explain.

ANNA

(Smiles insinuatingly) I've only heard what women say ...

FEDYA

Women! So it's not only Emma.

ANNA

He tries with every woman he meets—short, tall, blonde, dark, young, old. He is a true democrat. He believes that all women are created equal.

FEDYA

And they talk about him?

ANNA

Women talk about men.

FEDYA

They don't talk about me. Well, maybe I haven't done anything worth talking about. What do they say about Reitman?

ANNA

They say he makes love like a lion. (She growls at Fedya.)

VITO

Does that make up for the fact that he is a liar and a cheat?

FEDYA

Of course.

ANNA

Keep in mind that he goes everywhere with Emma, facing the police, the mobs.

VITO

Yes, all true, but he is a circus performer, a clown. He seeks all sensations.

ANNA

He didn't seek that incident in San Diego, where that mob kidnapped him and tortured him, almost killed him. He continued even after that. That shows some courage.

VITO

His courage is all in his sex organ.

FEDYA

Then his courage must be colossal.

ANNA

Oh, quiet! (She listens.) I hear someone on the stairs. (Emma enters, embraces everyone, sits down, smoking as she often does. It is winter. She removes her coat.)

EMMA

Someone out of the penitentiary today brought me a letter from Sasha. It's not a trick. It's his writing.

VITO

Well?

EMMA

Sasha has been in and out of the basket cell—it is too horrible to talk about. He refuses to bow down, so they punish him, again and again. Someone else would be dead.

FEDYA

You know Sasha. He's a bull.

EMMA

In his heart, yes. But he is flesh and blood. Even with good time, he has five years left. He has seen his friends die, one by one. Some die of sickness. Some hang themselves in their cells. He says he will not last five more years. (Fedya, agitated, gets up, paces. Emma pauses.) There is a reason he sent this letter with a friend. He has a plan. (She looks around.) Anna, is the door closed? (Anna checks, returns.) *A plan for escape.* (Everyone is listening. She keeps her voice down.) He says there is a vacant house one hundred yards outside the prison wall. It can be rented. A tunnel can be dug from the house, under the wall, up to an abandoned wash house in the yards, where he takes his walk.

VITO

A tunnel? Has Sasha gone out of his mind? I know what it takes to dig tunnels. It is impossible.

FEDYA

Poor Sasha. He has lost his senses.

ANNA

Is it so crazy?

VITO

Yes, completely crazy. It is impossible to do without being detected. It is a noisy operation. It takes more equipment than we have, more money than we have, more people than we have. More time than we have. Yes, it is completely crazy.

ANNA

What do you think, Emma?

EMMA

I think two things. First, it is, as Vito says, insane. In fact, impossible. And second … (She pauses.)

VITO

(Softly) And second, we must do it …

EMMA

Yes.

FEDYA

Yes.

ANNA

Yes, yes …

SCENE 4: LECTURE TOUR: EMMA AND BEN, EMMA AND ALMEDA

Reitman and Emma enter center stage, facing the audience. Ragtime music is the theme through the lecture tour.

REITMAN

Miss Goldman and I want to thank you for the hospitality you have shown us in Detroit. And now she is ready for your questions. (He cocks his ear.) The lady in the charming blue shawl wants to know: "Is it true that you believe in free love?" (He steps aside for Emma to come forward.)

EMMA

Free love? Of course. How can it be called love unless it is free? Is there anything more outrageous than the idea that a healthy grown woman, full of life and passion, must deny nature's demand, must subdue her most intense craving, break her spirit, stunt her vision, abstain from the depth and glory of sex until some so-called good man comes along to take her unto himself in marriage? Love, the strongest and deepest element in all life, the harbinger of hope, of joy, of ecstasy, love the defier of all laws, of all conventions, how can such an all-compelling force be synonymous with that pitiful product of state and church—marriage!

VOICE

Miss Goldman, are you against marriage?

EMMA

I am against all institutions that demand subservience. What a world it will be when men and women cast off the church, cast off the state, refuse to sacrifice their children to the monster of war, and come together in love! (Clattering of horses' hooves. Shouts. Reitman whispers in Emma's ear. She raises her hands.) I understand the police have surrounded the meeting hall. Please be calm. Please ... (Lights down. Lights up again on Reitman, facing the audience. Music signals a new situation.)

REITMAN

Dear friends in Los Angeles, Miss Emma Goldman's subject tonight is: "Patriotism."

EMMA

(Coming forward) Brothers and sisters, what is patriotism? Those who have had the fortune of being born on some particular spot consider themselves better, and nobler than the living beings inhabiting any other spot. It is, therefore, the duty of everyone living on that chosen spot to fight, kill, and die to impose his superiority upon all the others. Patriotism is the nourishment of war. And war is a quarrel between two thieves too cowardly to fight their own battle; therefore they take boys from one village and another village, stick them into uniforms, equip them with guns, and let them loose like wild beasts against each other. Listen to Tolstoy, who said: Free yourself from the obsolete idea of patriotism and from obedience to governments. Boldly enter the region of that higher idea, the brotherly union of all people, that idea which has come to life and from all sides is calling to you. (Applause.)

REITMAN

(Coming forward) Are there any questions? (He listens.) The gentleman in the back asks: "Does not patriotism make us a united people?"

EMMA

Yes, it unites us, *against* others. It intoxicates us, and drives us to violence against anyone different from us ... you need only look to the recent incident in San Diego, where a labor organizer, Joseph Mikolasek, a member of the I.W.W.—Industrial Workers of the World, how unpatriotic to be of the world!—Joseph Mikolasek was apprehended by two policemen. One had a gun, the other an axe. Together they shot and hacked Mikolasek to death. My manager and friend, Ben Reitman, dared to voice his indignation at that murder, whereupon some patriotic businessmen, pillars of the San Diego community, took him out to a deserted field, beat him, stripped him nude, threatened him with death, covered him with boiling tar, and used a red hot branding iron to burn into his bare skin the hated letters I.W.W. Such are the results of patriotism!

VOICE

The newspapers say Reitman invented that story.

EMMA

Dr. Reitman, you are accused of fabricating that incident. Do you want to reply?

REITMAN

(Coming forward, head high, facing the audience) Are there reporters present? Are there photographers present? Here is my reply ... (He turns, back to audience, and drops his pants—you see black scars on his backside—he quickly pulls up his pants.) I challenge you newspapermen to place this photo alongside the face of the governor of California, and let your readers decide which picture is more attractive. (Laughter, applause.)

EMMA

(Coming forward) Thank you for coming tonight. The meeting is adjourned. (She walks off quickly as the lights go down, then come up again on Emma and Ben, sitting at a table. She is drinking tea. He is eating voraciously. She is furious.) Ben, you are preposterous! You embarrass me continually. You embarrass our movement. It took all my willpower to just close the meeting after your performance. Sometimes I think you will never grow up.

REITMAN

(Shrugging) Emma, it was a joke. You and your comrades are too serious. Let's be more cheerful, less intense. It was just a joke, and to make a serious point.

EMMA

I'm not talking only about that exhibition tonight. What about last week, when that lovely old couple gave us bed and board in Detroit, and you came down to breakfast stark naked? And that meeting with the anarchist organizers in the Bronx—out of nowhere you started talking about God and Jesus ... And look at the outlandish way you dress. And the way you eat! (He has been gobbling his food, wiping his mouth on his arm.)

REITMAN

I eat as I do everything else, for enjoyment, not to obey the rules of etiquette. In short, my darling, I, unlike you, eat like an anarchist. (He emphasizes this by stuffing the last bit of food in his mouth.)

EMMA

You seem to think that anarchism has no respect for any of the ordinary niceties of behavior, like eating with some delicacy. Like bathing regularly.

REITMAN

Bathing?

EMMA

Yes, most people bathe.

REITMAN

Am I unbearable as I am? We have an hour before we catch our train. Do you really want me to spend half of it bathing? You know an hour with you is never enough, my darling. (He wipes his mouth, stands up, pulls her to her feet, takes off her shawl gently, kisses her passionately on the throat. She does not respond at first, but he continues. She turns and throws her arms around him.) You spoke wonderfully tonight, Emma. (He continues to kiss her, to touch her.)

EMMA

My God, Ben, I can't be angry with you. (He keeps kissing her, buries his head in her chest.) My God, Ben! My God!

REITMAN

I will yet convert you to Christianity, my sweetheart. (He kisses her again as the lights go down.)

Ragtime music. Lights up. Emma facing audience, holds up her hand for silence.

EMMA

Brothers and sisters, the San Francisco police have said I cannot speak here tonight. There are three thousand people in this hall, and if you are here to listen to me, then, police or no police, I am here to speak to you. This past month, I have gone from city to city in this nation that calls itself a democracy, speaking at sixteen meetings. Eleven were broken up by the police. We should all know by now that the

Constitution of the United States does not *give* us freedom of speech—that cannot be *given*, it must be *taken*. By people who insist on speaking, as I insist on speaking here tonight. (Applause. She looks out into the audience.) The young man here has a question.

VOICE

The newspapers say you are here in San Francisco because the fleet is in the harbor and you intend to blow it up.

EMMA

No, I think I will not blow up the fleet on this visit. (Laughter.) Bombs are not my way. But I would be happy to see the fleet sink quietly to the bottom of the sea, indeed, to see all warships everywhere in the world sink to the bottom of the sea, so that we, and our brothers and sisters in other countries, can live in peace. (Applause.)

Ragtime music. Lights up on Emma and Reitman in a corner of the stage, presumably in the back of a meeting hall. Her back is to him. She is obviously wrought up.

REITMAN

I was just being pleasant to her.

EMMA

You were leading her on.

REITMAN

Not seriously. I was just playing.

EMMA

(Turning around, furious) Don't you understand that it is wrong to play with another human being? Have you no sense of fairness or justice? Not only to me, but to these other women? I really don't know why I don't say goodbye to you once and for all. It is such hypocrisy, me speaking all over the country about women imprisoned by men, and then unable to tear myself away from you!

REITMAN

Don't berate yourself. It's my fault. My weakness. It was just one night.

EMMA

(Enraged) So you did spend the night! You liar! You said: "I can't be in Chicago and not see my mother." You spent the night with that woman. (She is beside herself, starts punching Reitman. He grabs her arms.) You liar!

REITMAN

Please, Emma, stop that. I have to introduce you in two minutes. Calm down. We'll talk afterward, my darling.

EMMA

We'll *fuck* afterward, my darling! No, not this time! Get out there and do your introduction. And don't wait for me at the hotel afterward. The committee will find me a place to stay. (Ben shakes his head ruefully, goes to face the audience, wiping his forehead with his kerchief.)

REITMAN

(Moving center stage to address the audience) Dear friends in New Kensington. What a pleasure to be in the beautiful state of Pennsylvania. I give you Miss Emma Goldman, speaking on: "The Drama of Henrik Ibsen." (Applause.)

EMMA

My brothers and sisters. (She glances at Reitman angrily, then composes herself.) We all know that in the home, not everything can be said. We know that in the factory, or wherever one works for a boss, not everything can be said. But on the stage, one can speak freely. And so the drama can be used to conquer ignorance, fear, prejudice. There are ignorance and prejudice about the most fundamental things of life. I am speaking of love and marriage. What does love have to do with marriage? The answer is: nothing. The wife, like the prostitute, is a commodity to be bought, the prostitute for a night, the wife for much longer. (Shouts of anger from the audience: "You are the whore!" "Who invited you?" "Get her off the stage!") Yes, the truth is hard to listen to. The man I have made so angry there in the first row is probably a husband who doesn't want his wife to hear her own secret thoughts spoken aloud. (Shout: "I'm getting out of here.") I'm sorry to see you go, sir. I wish you could hear about Henrik Ibsen. Ibsen's great play, *A Doll's House*, is about a woman, Nora. She has been living for eight years with a stranger. In a lovely house. A doll's house. But she has come to a decision. She is not a doll. She is a woman. And who is this stranger she has been living with? Her husband. Is it degrading for a prostitute to sleep for a night with a stranger? Then how degrading is an intimacy between two strangers, man and wife, which lasts a lifetime? Let us be careful, then, before we denounce prostitutes, before we brand them with that scarlet letter, because they are very much like women, for whom we should have compassion as they struggle for their souls, their bodies, their freedom. (Applause. Lights dim.)

Lights up on Emma and Almeda Sperry sitting at a kitchen table. She is a good-looking woman in her mid-thirties, dressed somewhat flamboyantly, wearing makeup.

ALMEDA

All right, I'll call you Emma. And you call me Almeda. Sperry's my last name, but no one round here knows it. It was so goddamn thrilling tonight to hear you talk about Ibsen. I have read *A Doll's House* three times. But I never could find anyone to talk with about it.

EMMA

I noticed you in the audience. I thought, that pretty woman, sitting there so rapt, looks like an actress.

ALMEDA

No, not me. But I love everything on stage. I almost committed suicide because Sarah Bernardt was coming here and I was broke. But a guy gave me a dollar. I won't tell you what I gave him. But it was worth it. I sat up in goose heaven and cried every time she spoke her lines.

EMMA

You live here alone?

ALMEDA

I have a husband—that's Fred. He calls himself my husband, but I don't think he is. He's not around much. No one worth talking about. How about you?

EMMA

I have a sweetheart. No one worth talking about. (They laugh.)

ALMEDA

That fella who introduced you? A handsome devil.

EMMA

Devil. That's the right word.

ALMEDA

Yeah, I know men like that. I could tell you stories all night.

EMMA

I'd like to hear them. I could learn a few things.

ALMEDA

And you tell me about Shaw and Strindberg. Never could find anything they wrote. Hey, I'll make some hot tea—got biscuits, too. I'd offer some booze but I drank it all before the meeting. That's my weakness. Well, not the only one. I know about handsome devils. Believe me, Emma, there's hardly anything anyone can tell me about men. I don't dare tell you how many men I have been with. And I'm still waiting to meet a *man*. Not just a biped who thinks he's a man because he has this thing.

EMMA

I do know a real man. He's in prison.

ALMEDA

I heard about him. It happened right here in Pennsylvania. Pittsburgh. Frick. The strike. I heard. Do you visit him?

EMMA

(Shaking her head) They won't let me near him.

ALMEDA

How long has it been?

EMMA

Nine years. (They are silent, sip their tea.)

ALMEDA

Does he know about your sweetheart?

EMMA

Yes and no.

ALMEDA

I know what you mean. Jealousy is strange. Fred is jealous of my friend Florence, who is Irish, French, and Jewish. She is beautiful, has dark hair and soft hands. She thinks that a woman should have each kid by a different man. That's what she thinks of marriage. What you said about marriage and prostitution, I couldn't believe you were saying it out loud. I have thought that for years. Men have used me, Emma. And I have used men. Just because I was short of money. You were saying the truth.

EMMA

I'm not saying something new. Just things people have been afraid to say in public.

ALMEDA

You do say it. I wish I could talk like that. I think I could, though, if not for drinking too much. But I need it with this lousy life—not just my life, but all around, people climbing up that steep hill so tired, slipping back, but climbing. You know why I married Fred? Hey! Your eyes are closing. God, I didn't think how tired you must be coming all night on the Pennsylvania Railroad, then talking your guts out. And tomorrow, I heard you say you got to be in New York for the big demonstration—the depression has hit New York bad, just like here. And I am going on like this … You go to bed, Emma …

EMMA

(Waking up) No, I'm listening. Please …

ALMEDA

You sure? I was saying how I got to marry Fred. It was to get out of my mother's house because it was so cold. She would never turn up the gas for fear of a big bill. And I was sick, coughing, and Fred took me out of there, and so I'm grateful to him, though he has lacerated my soul. (Emma is falling off again. Almeda walks over behind and gently massages her back and neck. Emma opens her eyes and clasps Almeda's hand as the lights go down.)

SCENE 5: UNION SQUARE

Emma appears center stage, revolutionary music in the background. She gets up on a box, to address an enormous crowd of the unemployed. Her style here is different than the lecture platform. This is a rally.

EMMA

Look around, my friends, look around! Thousands of working men and working women have come here today to Union Square to declare their anger at this system, which has no jobs for people willing to work. All over the city, the lines of the unemployed stretch for miles. In the richest city in the world! Yes, the richest city in the world, and women must sell their bodies just to stay alive! The richest city in the world, and children are crying for food. (A group of shabbily dressed men and women gather around her, as if her talk is a magnet, drawing them in. They are humming "Mein Greeneh Kuzine.") We ask for work, and they tell us to wait. We ask for medicine for the sick, and they tell us to pray. We ask for food, and they tell us to vote. (Police appear suddenly.) We ask for time to pay the rent, and they send the police. Yes, the police are here, as always, to protect the rich. Brothers and sisters. (Her tone rises.) If the children need milk, let us go into the stores and take it. If families need bread, let us find out where the flour is stored and take it. (The police move toward her.) Take it! Take it! (Police grab her roughly, and pull her off the platform as the lights go down and the hoof beats of the police horses get louder.)

SCENE 6: J. EDGAR HOOVER

Two men in a darkened office, the better to view photos, which are illumined by a spotlight. One man is slim, well-dressed, striped suit, lawyer-like—this is Attorney General Thomas Gregory. The other, a young man, stocky, hair slicked back, is J. Edgar Hoover, who is showing the photos—but he won't be identified until the very end of the scene. As they go through the photos, perhaps a projection of each appears on a screen for the audience.

HOOVER

(Showing a photo) This was last September.

GREGORY

What was she charged with?

HOOVER

Trespassing. She had brought women into the Smokers' Club in Minneapolis. A men's club.

GREGORY

A brazen one, isn't she? What is that sign she is carrying outside the club?

HOOVER

It says: "I am a heavy smoker."

GREGORY

I understand she travels everywhere with a man younger than herself.

HOOVER

Yes, his name is Reitman. He manages lectures. Our informants tell us that they have engaged in numerous immoral sexual acts. Never overt enough to make an arrest.

GREGORY

(Taking another photo in his hands) What is this one?

HOOVER

New York City, the Lower East Side. It was a meeting of Jewish women. She told them how to use contraceptives.

GREGORY

How much time did she get for that?

HOOVER

She was released for lack of evidence. It seems she spoke to the group entirely in the Jewish language, and our informant could not understand a word.

GREGORY

Is this the lot?

HOOVER

No, sir. This is a partial record. She has been arrested fourteen times.

GREGORY

Where is she now?

HOOVER

She is serving a one-year sentence on Blackwell's Island. Inciting to riot.

GREGORY

But she'll be out soon and back to her old tricks. Just as the situation in Cuba is getting serious.

HOOVER

We are looking for a way to deport her. Back to Russia.

GREGORY

That would be ideal. But I understand she was married once to an American citizen.

HOOVER

Yes, when she was seventeen. To one Jacob Kershner, a naturalized citizen, and so she automatically became a citizen under the law.

GREGORY

Well, our laws were not intended to make the country helpless before its enemies.

HOOVER

We are working on the problem, sir.

GREGORY

I'm glad to hear that.

HOOVER

It is a challenge. We are dealing with the most dangerous woman in America.

GREGORY

Thank you, Mr. Hoover.

SCENE 7: EMMA IN PRISON

Emma, center stage, sitting on her prison cot, writing. In three different parts of the stage, by turns in darkness or lighted, sit Sasha, in prison uniform, Reitman, in characteristic garb, and Almeda Sperry. They all speak out their own letters.

SASHA

My dearest Emma ... I heard that your speech in Union Square was magnificent, and that you have been sentenced to a year in Blackwell's Island. Please take care of yourself ... The guards found an escape tunnel—they didn't know who was responsible but they decided to punish me anyway—the stomach pump every morning, the straitjacket every night. For seven days and nights. I lost consciousness, I don't know for how long. But I woke up this morning and heard a sparrow singing outside my window, and thought: I must be alive.

EMMA

My darling Ben ... I am ashamed and horrified because of what has become of me since I met you. Sasha risked his life, surrendered his freedom, for all of us. I wrote him that I couldn't sleep all night thinking of him. That was a lie. Most of the night I lie awake thinking of you. Thinking of that first night in Chicago when you aroused me as no man has ever aroused me, when you took me like a hurricane and I forgot everything and everybody.

REITMAN

You know I love Sasha as you do. Don't torment yourself. Life is what it is. Love is what it is. How I wish I could be with you, to massage your tired body, to kiss every inch of it.

EMMA

Last night, I lay in my cot trembling, my throat choked, as it always is when we come together, in that moment before your first embrace.

REITMAN

I want to be with you. Gloom has my soul. I am afraid you will forget.

EMMA

Darling Ben ... Why do I think so much of you? I should be thinking of the work that must be done when I get out of here. The country is going mad over Cuba. I do think of these things. But very soon your image appears and crowds out everything else. How I want you! I want to devour you.

REITMAN

You are my whole world. How terrible it is to love.

EMMA

I sometimes get angry. I think of your infidelities, your rotten infidelities, your lies, your excuses. And then I lie back, my eyes closed, and I forget everything for want of you ...

ALMEDA

Dearest Emma ... Fred is angry with me tonight because I gave a bucket of soup and a loaf of homemade bread to my friend Irene. She runs a stock company here in the summer and plays in little jerkwater towns in the winter. How are you, my dear moonbeam shimmering on a dark pool at night, my drop of dew hidden in the heart of a wild rose?

EMMA

Accept my love for what it is, and for what it cannot be. But it is there, and real.

ALMEDA

How sweet of you to say the things you said to me in your last letter. Yes, I remember that wonderful day-evening -night-morning we had together in between your Pittsburgh speech and your Philadelphia rally. It made me stop drinking. Then my mother died. We never did get along, but when she was near gone, I went to see her. I kissed her hand, and she began to cry. When she left this earth, it rained all day and I drank and drank.

EMMA

Don't ask, as you once did, am I, Almeda, really a socialist or anarchist, or what am I? It doesn't matter. Just do what your instincts tell you, be what you are so naturally, so honest, so direct, so impossible to give a name to.

ALMEDA

Dear Emma ... I'll never forget the day you took me in your arms and I kissed your beautiful throat, the throat of a bird I once saw. Your eyes are like violets in the morning. I know your work comes first, the cause comes first, but when your term is up, I will come to see you wherever you are. Some days I want a baby so bad, don't you? You told me once you did. You told me how you thought you were having one and then it was a mistake. That was the first time I ever saw you cry.

REITMAN

Dearest Emma ... I'm going to Pennsylvania tomorrow to sell some good literature and organize a fund for political prisoners. I will look up your friend in New Kensington. I think she is on the sponsoring committee for my talk ...

ALMEDA

Dear Emma ... Your boyfriend Reitman came to New Kensington. He is a strange bird. Some day I'll tell you about it.

Sound of steel doors clanging. Voice: "Goldman! Goldman!" Lights down. Then up again, as clanging of steel doors continues, then stops. A woman—she could be a Black or a white woman in her forties, definitely Southern—is sitting and sewing her nurse's smock. A matron brings in Emma, who can barely walk, and who sits down immediately on a cot.

MATRON

Lizbeth, here's a new helper for you. She's just outa solitary. The warden says to teach her good, keep her out of trouble. (She leaves.)

LIZBETH

(Goes over to Emma, who is hunched over.) Now don't sit squinched up like that. You not in solitary any more. You better start using your legs, else you'll never be able to walk again. Now get up. (She pulls her up and helps her walk in a tiny circle while continuing to talk.) What they got you in solitary for? (She looks into Emma's face.) No need to tell me. You're that Red Emma they talk about. They say you don't take sass from no one. They say you put in charge of the sewing room and they wanted you get the girls working faster and you wouldn't, no-how. (She laughs.) Yeah, I hear them talk about you. They say you want to change the whole world … I hear somethin' else. I hear you got a handsome boyfriend brings you home-bake cookies, and you give them out to everybody. Now see here, Emma, I just love home-bake cookies! (She laughs. Emma smiles weakly. She is beginning to come alive.) You know me? (Emma shakes her head.) I'm Lizbeth. I'm the prison nurse. They wants you to help me in the hospital ward. And I'm goin' to teach you all kinds of things. Startin' right now. Lay yourself down. Like this. (Gently pushes her down. She massages Emma's legs.) You got to know when to make people walk, and when to make them keep still. You got to know when to rub hard, and when to rub gentle. You got to know when to use a cold compress, and when to use a hot one. Hey, why do they call you Red Emma?

EMMA

It's a long story.

LIZBETH

We got lots o' time in here. (She laughs at this ancient prison joke.) You tell me about that, and I'll tell you what to do when a woman starts bleeding down there ... You ever bring a baby into the world? (Emma shakes her head.) Emma, you bring someone's baby into the world, and you can do just about anything. Next week, there's a girl up in the ward about to have her birth. And you are goin' to help me. (She takes Emma's wrist and puts her fingers on her pulse.) Now first thing, I'm goin' to teach you to take a pulse. You put your fingers here (she holds out her wrist). Feel that? That's my life, beatin' for you. Won't stop no matter what. Goes on beatin', on and on. Isn't that beautiful? (She looks into Emma's face.) You want to learn nursing, Emma?

EMMA

I want you to teach me, Lizbeth.

LIZBETH

I will teach you. Now I want you to remember one thing.

EMMA

What?

LIZBETH

I just *love* home-bake cookies! (She laughs uproariously, Emma manages a smile, as the scene ends.)

SCENE 8: SPEECH AT THALIA THEATER ON RELEASE

Music from Verdi. Shouts: "Welcome home Emma!" Singing. Emma comes on stage, to address her friends at the Thalia Theater, greeting her return from prison. She is low-key, a little pale.

EMMA

It's strange. Do you know, I tried two years ago to investigate prison conditions. They wouldn't let me near a prison. Then, suddenly, a stroke of luck. (She smiles.) I was inside! (Shakes her head.) Oh, I learned so much in this year on Blackwell's Island. And what I learned I'll never forget. (She pauses.) Being there made me think, even more than before, about our comrade Alexander Berkman. (Applause.) And all the others who fill the prisons. (She chokes up a little, remembering.) And I promised myself, day after day inside that hell, listening to the other women, marveling, as I took their pulses, that their hearts could beat so strongly in defiance of their condition ... I promised myself that I would not rest until the prisons of this country are taken apart, brick by brick, and the iron bars melted down, to make playgrounds for our children ... It's good to be back with you, my brothers and sisters ... (Music rises, fades.)

SCENE 9: BIRTH—EMMA AND HELENA

Music recalls family scene. Emma comes, with a lighted candle, into a darkened room.

EMMA

Helena, my darling sister, where are you? Don't you have any light?

HELENA

Here—I'm in bed. I ran out of kerosene last week. I'm so glad you're here. I haven't seen you since Papa passed away. And I had to bring you that news.

EMMA

It was strange. I had so often cursed him, wished he were dead. But then, when it happened, I thought: he was just a working man, his life was hard, and his cruelty was the cruelty of his own life.

HELENA

It was right after that you went to Europe.

EMMA

To Vienna. To learn to be a midwife.

HELENA

I was so excited to hear that. I thought, I want Emma to bring out my baby, no one else. Am I your first?

EMMA

(Shakes her head.) In Vienna, I delivered six babies. No, seven. One woman had twins. And just last week on the East Side. The woman was so sick. It was a foul and miserable room. But she gave birth to a beautiful black-haired baby. You should have seen it, Helena. It came out with clenched fists. What a fighter!

HELENA

A boy?

EMMA

A girl. (They both laugh.) How far along are you?

HELENA

Maybe seven months. You can see ...

EMMA

Yes. (Peers at her) You have good color in your face. (She takes her wrist.) Your pulse is regular. (She touches her.) Does this hurt?

HELENA

No, it feels good.

EMMA

Now let me listen. (She places her stethoscope against Helena's uterus.)

HELENA

What are you listening for?

EMMA

Sssshh!

HELENA

You're listening for the heartbeat. You hear it?

EMMA

Don't talk now. (She listens.)

HELENA

Do you hear it? You should hear it!

EMMA

We'll try again in a few minutes. Sometimes it takes a while. Now just relax. Tell me about Mama.

HELENA

Mama's all right. She sits all day and sews. How's Sasha? Did they ever let you see him?

EMMA

(Shakes her head, then turns her face away to control herself.) Sasha was sure he would not come out alive. We were desperate. Our comrades began to dig a tunnel. It's hard to believe. Such a crazy idea. But they did it. They were inches away from the prison yard, and it was discovered. A really crazy idea. But it almost worked. They weren't sure it was for Sasha, but they punished him anyway. (She closes her eyes, then shakes it off.)

HELENA

Is it true there's another man you are with?

EMMA

Yes. A sensitive, beautiful man—on Mondays, Wednesdays, Fridays. On Tuesday, Thursday, Saturday, Sunday—an insensitive monster. (Sighs.) Helena, have you ever been so infatuated, so physically infatuated with a man, that it made you insane?

HELENA

Just the opposite. For me it was the absence of such a feeling that made me insane. You know my marriage …

EMMA

Yes.

HELENA

But I do want this child. So much. Emma, try again.

EMMA

(Applying the stethoscope again, listening …) Sometimes …

HELENA

I'm nervous, Emma! You know I've lost two. I want this baby so much. You understand. You love children. I hope you have a child some day, Emma.

EMMA

You know my condition.

HELENA

But the doctors said: an operation …

EMMA

Doctors! One had me believing last year I was pregnant. For two months I believed it. How happy I was! Then the same doctor, very calm, said: "Oh, a mistake!" I wanted to kill her. I cried for a week. No one knew. I just disappeared for a whole week and cried.

HELENA

You'll have the operation, then.

EMMA

No. A woman has the right to decide not to have children, doesn't she?

HELENA

Of course, but ...

EMMA

Now I'm a midwife. I can bring all kinds of children into the world. That makes me happy. (She places the stethoscope again.) Ssshh! (She hands the ear piece to Helena, who listens.)

HELENA

I hear something ...

EMMA

That's your baby. A strong, strong beat.

HELENA

(Throwing her arms around Emma) Oh my God!

EMMA

Come, let's walk. It's good for you and your baby. (They start to walk around the room.) You know, Helena, I'm going to bring a million little babies into the world. And as they come out of their mothers' wombs, I will whisper in their tiny ears: "Rebel! Rebel! Join together! Change the world!" And in one generation ...

HELENA

Emma! Don't you get arrested before my time comes!

SCENE 10: PRESIDENT MCKINLEY: REPORTERS AND EMMA

Band music, darkness. McKinley's speech is on tape.

VOICE

Fellow citizens, the President of the United States! (Band strikes up.)

MCKINLEY

My fellow Americans ... I am indeed happy to be present at this splendid Exposition in the historic city of ... (he pauses to remember) Buffalo. It is a pleasure to report to you that our great nation is in good health. Business is prospering. Overseas, our war with Spain has yielded the most happy results. War is always to be regretted. But Cuba is now free and under our protection. Puerto Rico is ours. Hawaii fell like a ripe fruit into our arms. I did puzzle for some time on what to do with the Philippines, and then I got down on my knees and prayed to God, and he said: "Take them, Mr. President. Civilize them, Christianize them ..." And so ... (A shot is heard. Silence.)

Lights up on reporters milling about, notebooks in hand. Reitman appears, in his usual get-up.)

REITMAN

Gentlemen, she will be here in a moment. (Emma walks on stage, immediately surrounded by the reporters.)

REPORTER

Miss Goldman, after President McKinley was shot, why did they arrest *you?*

EMMA

You are reporters. You know the police don't need evidence to arrest someone. The President was assassinated. A government always goes into a frenzy when someone else uses its own tactic. (Her mood is calm, good-humored in all this.)

REPORTER

Its own tactic?

EMMA

Murder.

REPORTER

Radical organizations all over the country have repudiated the assassin Czolgosz. It is said that you defend him.

EMMA

I defend not his act, but his anguish.

REPORTER

Do you believe Czolgosz is insane?

EMMA

He must be. He killed one man, with no force of law behind him. If he were the President of the United States, he could do as McKinley did, send an army into the Philippines to kill ten-year-old children. That would be legal. And perfectly sane.

REPORTER

Is it true you offered to nurse the President after he was wounded?

EMMA

Yes. (A hint of a smile.) But for some reason, my offer was not accepted.

REPORTER

Then you felt compassion for the President?

EMMA

Of course. You must feel compassion for a President who doesn't know where the Philippines are until the merchants and bankers point it out to him on the map.

REPORTER

You are quoted as saying that business interests benefited from the war.

EMMA

I know one thing. The working classes got nothing from it. They never do. Their sons died on those islands. And when the smoke of battle was gone, and the dead buried, the cost of the war came home to the families of the dead, in higher prices for food and rent.

REPORTER

Your friend Berkman is in prison for an attempted assassination. Does he approve of what Czolgosz did?

EMMA

When he is released from prison, you can ask him yourself. But I can tell you that neither Berkman nor I believe, as some of us once did, that assassination is a step toward revolution.

REPORTER

Have you decided then that the way to change is through the ballot box?

EMMA

The ballot box! Voting is a game to keep everyone busy while the rich take control of the nation's wealth. When Rockefeller wants an oil refinery, does he take a vote? When McKinley wants the Philippines, does he take a vote?

REPORTER

Then what do you propose?

EMMA

People will organize, wherever they work, wherever they live. And when they are strong enough, they will take back this country, take back everything that was stolen from them. It's much simpler than voting.

REPORTER

(As the scene ends with ragtime music) Can we quote you on all this?

EMMA

(Smile) Will your newspapers print all this? (Music louder, Reitman takes her by the arm as the lights go down.)

SCENE 11: SASHA RETURNS: SACHS' CAFE

Railroad station. Spring. Dusk. Railroad whistle. Sound of engine starting up, train moving away. A man is standing, back to audience, stage right, wearing a hat, an oversized coat, carrying a small suitcase. He is motionless. Emma comes in stage left, stops. She is carrying flowers. She sees the man, studies him a moment, then calls hesitantly: "Sasha?" The man doesn't move at first. Then he turns and looks at her, remains where he is. She takes some steps toward him, stops. He doesn't answer. She moves to him. He nods his head. She throws her arms around him and they embrace, in silence, then break away. She holds out the flowers. He takes them, closes his eyes, presses his lips against the flowers. Lights down.

Lights up on Sachs' Cafe. A reprise of the Sachs' Cafe music. Vito and Anna arrive, and sit down at a table. They are better dressed than in the old days. They are fourteen years older.

VITO

(Calling out) Mr. Sachs! (Turns to Anna) It's still the same service. (Mr. Sachs arrives.)

SACHS

Vito! Anna! After all these years! (He grasps their hands.) Vito, you're still complaining. But it's good to see you back. Tell me, do you still work in the sewers?

VITO

Do I look like a man who works in the sewers?

SACHS

(Looks him over carefully.) You look more prosperous. You look like a man who once worked in the sewers.

VITO

You are a perceptive man, Mr. Sachs. I have risen in the world. I am a bookkeeper for the Sewer Department.

SACHS

Hmmm. Who would believe that the Sewer Department keeps books? And you, Anna?

ANNA

I'm not in the factory any more. I'm an organizer for the garment union.

SACHS

Still *toomeling*. I knew it. Tell me, have I changed?

VITO

A little more grey in your hair. A little more distinguished looking. But your tablecloths are the same. Don't you think, after fourteen years, you should change the tablecloths?

SACHS

(Sighs) The same Vito. A wonderful person. Just a little crazy. How about a little wine to sober you up? I know it's a special day. Where are the others?

ANNA

Here comes the wine! (Fedya has arrived, carrying a bottle. He is dressed elegantly. She and Vito get up and embrace Fedya. Sachs, standing off, observes Fedya.)

SACHS

Beautiful! Beautiful!

FEDYA

Good to see you, Mr. Sachs. (Shakes his hand.) How about some glasses? You'll drink with us.

SACHS

Like old times. You bring your own wine. I supply the glasses. It's a miracle I'm still in business.

ANNA

(Excitedly) They're here! (Emma and Sasha have arrived. Anna gets up, goes to Sasha. They embrace.)

SASHA

Anna! Dear Anna! (He is not the old, strong-looking, confident

Sasha. He is a little bent, more subdued in manner. He turns and embraces Vito, then looks and sees Fedya. Fedya brushes a tear from his eye, comes over and embraces Sasha, then Emma. Vito pulls chairs over for them. They sit down. Sachs comes in with a tray of glasses.)

SACHS

(Putting down the tray, he grasps Sasha's hand.) Sasha! Sasha! So good to see you. So many years. What you have been through! Have something to eat. It's my treat.

SASHA

(Shakes his head, speaks quietly.) I'm not hungry, Mr. Sachs. I'll just sit a while.

SACHS

This is something new, Sasha refusing food! I never ...

EMMA

Enough, Mr. Sachs.

SACHS

What did I say? Did I say something wrong?

VITO

It's all right, Mr. Sachs. Nothing wrong. (Turns to Sasha) Sasha, you should have some food.

EMMA

Don't tell him what to do, Vito. (They are all on edge.)

VITO

Don't do this, don't do that! Forgive me, Emma.

SACHS

Look. (He holds out a newspaper.) Look, in the afternoon paper, a picture of you Sasha, an old one. (He reads) "Alexander Berkman, Frick assailant, released after fourteen years." (Vito takes the paper, reads, looks up.)

VITO

There's something about you, too, Emma, on the opposite page. He hands it to her. (She reads.)

FEDYA

What is it?

EMMA

The government has revoked the citizenship of Jacob Kershner, my former husband. That means I am no longer a citizen. And so ... (She is pensive.) The hypocrites. How they play with the law.

ANNA

Will they try to deport you now, Emma?

EMMA

Perhaps. Or they will wait until I break some federal law.

FEDYA

It's too depressing. Let's drink a toast. To Sasha's return. (They all drink.)

SASHA

(Softly) Thank you, dear friends. I ... (He is interrupted by sounds from the street, marching music, singing. Sachs goes to the door.)

FEDYA

What is it, Mr. Sachs?

SACHS

(Still looking out into the street) I don't know. I see soldiers and sailors marching. (He calls out into the street) What's the parade? (Someone in the street responds. Sachs returns to the group. He is very solemn.) President Wilson has asked Congress to declare war on Germany. (Everyone is silent.)

FEDYA

First Europe goes mad. Now America.

ANNA

Congress will be voting very quickly. They become like sheep when a President asks for war. We have to move fast.

VITO

This was expected, Anna. A rally has been called for next week. At the Harlem River Casino. Emma is one of the speakers.

ANNA

Emma must not speak. Now with this news of Kershner and her citizenship, they will pounce on her in a minute.

EMMA

I cannot be silent now. If I cannot speak at a moment like this, everything I have done up to now is worthless.

FEDYA

Emma, it would be a mistake. (They are all silent.)

SASHA

(Speaking up for the first time, causing everyone to turn his way—he speaks softly.) Emma, I think Fedya is right. You can miss one meeting. I will speak in your place.

ANNA

(Alarmed) No, Sasha! Fourteen years is enough.

SASHA

They have silenced me all these years. It is time for me to speak. I must.

EMMA

(Putting her arms around Sasha) Let it be both of us. Sasha and I. We will both speak against the war. (Everyone is silent.)

SACHS

My dear friends. (He wipes a tear from his eye.) Let's open a bottle of wine. Sasha is back with us! (Lights down.)

SCENE 12: EMMA AND BEN PART

Music. Reitman and Emma in a room. He has just come in. She is clearly upset by his presence. Keeps her distance.

EMMA

Why did you come, Ben? You stayed away six months. And here you are, just before I am to speak. They are expecting six thousand people.

REITMAN

My darling! When I heard the news, that war was declared, I knew I must come to you. I am frightened for you, Emma. Today Wilson signs the Conscription Law, and tonight, anyone who speaks against it … You know what they want to do to you. Don't speak tonight.

EMMA

I don't need your advice.

REITMAN

Why so cold, my sweetheart? Why so utterly cold? What is going on? Is it because I can't join you in this? It's not my way. I don't believe in putting our heads into their nooses.

EMMA

Someone must. If we can only persist, we will be too many for their nooses.

REITMAN

Dreams, dreams, Emma. How I love your dreams. But I am afraid for you with your dreams. I can't stand the thought of you in prison again. And what if they send you out of the country? What would I do without you? You, my sweetheart, my Venus, my love!

EMMA

Enough, Ben. Your one concern is: what will *you* do?

REITMAN

Have I not stood with you? Have I not faced down howling mobs, from here to California?

EMMA

Yes. I never understood why. You were never one of us …

REITMAN

My God, so cold, Emma, so cold. What is wrong? Why can't we just be happy? You and your friends—they cannot stand joy. They cannot be at peace. Wilson declares war. You declare war. Why is that necessary? Let Wilson sign his Act. Let those who don't want to fight not fight. Why must we stand on platforms and exhort and push and trumpet our defiance? They are setting a trap for us, Emma. Be careful tonight. And think of Sasha. Can he survive another term in prison?

EMMA

You're not thinking of Sasha. You're thinking of yourself.

REITMAN

My darling, you're upset for some reason. (He reaches for her, she turns away, pulls a letter from her pocket.)

EMMA

I received a letter from Almeda Sperry.

REITMAN

Almeda Sperry ... I'm trying to remember ...

EMMA

What a bad memory my poor Ben has! Almeda Sperry. She met you when you went to speak in Pennsylvania.

REITMAN

(Suddenly remembering) Oh yes, that drunken socialist whore in New Kensington.

EMMA

(Angry) That drunken socialist whore! Who sold herself to men when she had nothing to eat. Who single-handedly built a socialist group in that godforsaken little town. The most straight-speaking person I have ever known.

REITMAN

More so than me?

EMMA

Listen. (She reads from the letter.) "Darling Emma, I am amused by Reitman. But don't ever send him to New Kensington again. I have had a deep horror of him ever since he met me at the railroad station. I understood him thoroughly as soon as he took my arm the way he did when we walked along the street. Please ask him, for the sake of the cause, if he ever goes to meet another sinful woman who is beginning to see a glimmer of light—please ask him, for humanity's sake, for his own sake, and the woman's sake, not to begin *fuck talk*."

REITMAN

She writes vividly … Truth is, I'm not sure what she's talking about.

EMMA

You are such a liar.

REITMAN

Have I ever denied it? I would be lying if I did, and why add one more to my long history? But how can one live in this world without lying, Emma?

EMMA

Lying to your enemies, perhaps. To those you love, that is unpardonable.

REITMAN

But that is what is wonderful about you, Emma. You have always pardoned the unpardonable.

EMMA

Yes, Ben. I have always pardoned everything in you. (She turns from him. He puts his arms around her, kisses her neck.) Oh, that first time you took me by the arm. How you took me by the arm! How angry I was! How thrilled I was! (She turns and embraces him.)

REITMAN

(Gently) I was not playing with you, Emma. I have stayed
with you, year after year. (She breaks away.)

EMMA

Yes, you have. On and off. Steadfast, and deceitful. You always made me forget everything else when I was with you. I
was ashamed of my craving for you, and yet I couldn't stop.
What a sham! I speak all over America about the independ-
ence of woman, and then I rush to you. You have made my
life so worth living, you bastard! (She presses against him,
grasps his hair as if to hurt him. He winces. She breaks away.)
I have to go, to speak. This is ridiculous!

REITMAN

Will we meet after you speak?

EMMA

No. Not tonight. Not any night. Not any more.

REITMAN

I will miss you, my blue-eyed darling.

EMMA

Will you be at the meeting?

REITMAN

I have a train ticket to Chicago. But I can wait until tomorrow
if only you and I ... (She shakes her head, starts to leave.)
Please, Emma, be careful tonight. Criticize Wilson. Condemn
the war. But there will be draft-age young men in the audi-

ence. If you urge them to refuse conscription, the government is ready to spring. We need you and Sasha …

EMMA

Goodbye, dear Ben. (She starts to leave, turns back, for a long, passionate kiss, then breaks off quickly and walks off without looking back. Reitman looks after her, then straightens his tie, picks up his cane, and walks off in the other direction.)

SCENE 13: HARLEM RIVER CASINO

Huge crowd. Taped crowd noises. Music. Emma and Sasha sitting on chairs, facing the audience.

SASHA

You said you wouldn't see Ben Reitman again.

EMMA

He came to me. (Sounds of crashing glass.)

SASHA

The sailors in the balcony. Look, they're unscrewing the light bulbs and … (Crash of light bulbs around them.)

EMMA

Ben and I are finished.

SASHA

But are you finished with … with what you wanted in him? (More crashing of glass light bulbs around them.)

EMMA

(Turns to look at Sasha) Never, Sasha. Never finished with *that.*

SASHA

You're being introduced. (They listen—Emma rises and faces the audience.)

EMMA

(Waits for crashing light bulbs to stop before she addresses the audience in a loud clear voice.) So this is the war to make the world safe for democracy! Thank you, friends in the balcony, for clarifying that. (Silence, then another crash, laughter. Emma points up to the balcony.) You, young man, put that down, and tell us what is on your mind.

VOICE FROM BALCONY

I was born in this country, and I'm willing to die for this country! (Yells of approval around him.)

EMMA

(Waits for noise to die down.) I, too, am willing to die for this country. (Silence. Her voice rises.) Yes, for this *country.* For the mountains and rivers, the land, the *people,* yes, for the *country.* But not for the President, not for the generals and admirals, not for the industrialists and bankers who want this war. *They* are not our country. They do not care a damn whether you, young man, live or die. What is patriotism, my friends? Is it love of your government? No, it is love of your country, of your fellow men and women. And that love, *that* patriotism, may require you to oppose your government. (Applause.) Mark this day, my friends. The 18th of May 1917. The president has signed the Conscription Law, and the young men of this nation will now be marched into the slaughterhouse of the war in Europe. I say to you, young men in the balcony, and young men everywhere: Refuse to die! Refuse to kill! If you have a mind of your own, a will of your own, if you do not want to be a slave of authority, if you believe in democracy and liberty and peace for all mankind, refuse, refuse! (Enormous applause, stamping of feet. Sasha is standing, applauding with the rest. Anna and Vito leap onto the stage to grasp Emma's hands.)

ANNA

Emma, the hall is full of federal agents!

VITO

They're coming down the aisle.

VOICE THROUGH MEGAPHONE

Clear the hall! By order of the United States government! No one leave the stage. Stay where you are. (Vito turns toward the voice and gives it the Italian gesture of defiance. Then he takes Emma's hand on one side, Sasha's on the other. Anna takes Sasha's hand. The four face the audience as the lights go down.)

The End

Books by Howard Zinn available from Haymarket Books

Disobedience and Democracy
Nine Fallacies on Law and Order

❧

Failure to Quit
Reflections of an Optimistic Historian

❧

Vietnam
The Logic of Withdrawal

❧

SNCC
The New Abolitionists

❧

The Southern Mystique

❧

Justice in Everyday Life
The Way It Really Works

❧

Postwar America
1945–1971

❧

Emma
A Play in Two Acts About Emma Goldman, American Anarchist

❧

Marx in Soho
A Play on History

order online from HaymarketBooks.org